U0095405

高校秘书学专业系列教材　总主编◎杨剑宇

涉外秘书英语听说

总主编◎杨剑宇　副总主编◎冯修文

主　编◎肖爱萍　朱向荣　副主编◎许　刚　严大为

编　者（排名不分先后）

李懿蔺　许　刚　严大为

朱向荣　肖爱萍

华东师范大学出版社

涉外秘书专业本科系列教材编委会

总　序

　　涉外秘书是指在我国三资企业、外国驻华机构、我国涉外单位和部门等供职,辅助上司实施涉外经济活动或涉外事务管理的专门人才,是改革开放后产生的新型的外向型秘书。

　　涉外秘书要求能精通外语,操作办公自动化设备,懂经济、法律,掌握秘书工作理论和技能,了解和适应不同的中外文化环境,具有国际眼光,熟悉国际市场游戏规则,适应国际竞争的需要。

　　我国高校的秘书专业诞生于1980年。1984年起,在广东、上海、北京先后产生了涉外秘书专业。当时,有的称中英文秘书,有的称现代秘书等等。1996年,教育部高等教育自学考试办公室将涉外秘书作为一个独立的自考专业设置。同时,在成人高校也设立了涉外秘书专业,先是专科,后发展的既有专科、也有本科;众多高校也设置了涉外秘书专业的本科方向。2012年,秘书学专业被教育部列入本科目录,涉外秘书专业迎来又一个发展高潮。

　　专业建设,教材领先。我从上世纪80年代中期起在上海任教涉外秘书专业课程,教材是自编的讲义。从90年代起的一二十年中,先后应华侨出版社、湖北科技出版社和上海人民出版社之约,在讲义的基础上修改补充,弃旧增新,出版了几批涉外秘书专业的教材,包括全国自考统考的涉外秘书专业教材,计有《涉外秘书概论》、《涉外秘书实务》、《秘书和公共关系》、《涉外秘书礼仪》、《涉外秘书英语》、《秘书英语》等。这些教材满足了高校师生教学的急需。但是,由于这几批教材是在讲义基础上产生的,难免存在局限性。尤其是,涉外秘书专业的根本特性是涉外性,外语是涉外秘书的基本功,而这些教材除《涉外秘书英语》、《秘书英语》外,全是中文写的。所以,我一直计划组织编写一套以英语为主的,更加适合实际需要的涉外秘书专业教材。

　　在全国百佳出版单位华东师范大学出版社和上海建桥学院的支持下,这一计划得以实现。我们组织了从事涉外秘书专业教学多年、具有丰富经验的一线教师,编写成了这套教材,计有7册:《涉外秘书导论》、《涉外秘书实务》、《涉外秘书英语综合》、《涉外秘书英语阅读》、《涉外秘书英语写作》、《涉外秘书英语听说》、《涉外商务单证》。除《涉外秘书导论》和《涉外秘书实务》是用中文写的外,其余均用英语撰写。

　　掌握一门外语,是担任涉外秘书的基本条件。由于英语在世界上最为流行,因此,涉外秘书应当熟练地掌握英语。熟练地掌握英语,包括准确地听懂,流利地说清,快速地阅读,熟练地书写和翻译。涉外秘书工作的实践证明,仅学习、掌握普通英语是不够的。要胜任涉外秘书工作,还必须学习、掌握涉外秘书工作的职业英语。为此,我们针对涉外秘书工作的实际需要,在调查了解涉外秘书实际工作的基础上,编写了本系列教材,以满足师生的需要。

本系列教材的编写,遵循三个原则:实用;由浅入深;训练听、说、读、写、译能力。

实用是指本系列教材内容紧紧围绕涉外秘书的主要业务,如接听电话、接待来访、安排上司工作日程和商务旅行、筹办会议以及处理邮件、传真,拟写社交书信、贸易信函、经济合同等,对这些业务,本系列教材具有直接的指导作用。

由浅入深是指本系列教材的布局先从最简单的运用英语接听电话等开始,继而逐步深入,做到由易到难,循序渐进。

训练听、说、读、写、译能力,指本系列教材内容既有接听电话、接待来访等以训练听说能力为主的单元,也有传真、拟写社交书信、贸易信函、经济合同等以训练读写译为主的单元,还有筹办会议、应聘等综合训练听、说、读、写、译能力的单元。

同时,我们还组织编写了秘书学本科专业系列教材,其中的《文书处理和档案管理》、《秘书应用写作》、《管理学原理》、《秘书公关原理与实务》、《中国秘书史》、《秘书心理学》等教材,涉外秘书专业可以通用。这样,这套教材实际上共有13册,是至今最完整的名副其实的涉外秘书本科系列教材。

在本系列教材的出版过程中,华东师范大学出版社的李恒平、范耀华和姚望三位编辑给予了很大帮助,在此谨表谢意。

我们付出了努力,希望把这套教材尽可能编得好些。但是,由于涉外秘书尚是发展中的专业,加之我们水平有限,本系列教材不足之处在所难免,敬请广大读者指正。

本系列教材得到上海市扶持基金项目资助。

杨剑宇

2013 年 2 月

前　　言

秘书学于2012年正式列入教育部本科目录,这是秘书界一件可喜可贺的大事。可喜之后,难免有点忧愁。那就是秘书学本科的教材建设,特别是秘书英语的教材建设。我们知道,教材作为"整个教育系统的软件",不仅反映着社会发展的要求,同时在某种程度上还直接决定着受教育者的培养质量。因而,世界各国都非常重视教材的开发和建设。今日之秘书人才培养,不能再局限于"办文、办会、办事"能力,而是要立足现代开放型经济对秘书岗位能力的需要。由此可见,我们培养出的涉外秘书本科人才,要具备较高的岗位英语应用能力,才能胜任其岗位需要,尤其是涉外企事业单位秘书岗位所需的英语应用能力,这是未来本科涉外秘书英语教材建设的重点。基于此,由上海建桥学院秘书系牵头,华东师范大学出版社组织国内从事涉外秘书英语教学的一线骨干教师和企业涉外秘书岗位从业人员共同编写了这套涉外秘书英语系列教材,丛书的核心理念旨在培养涉外秘书岗位所需的英语应用能力。

本教材是涉外秘书英语系列教材中的听说教程。全书共10个单元,旨在培养和提高涉外秘书岗位所需的沟通交际能力,内容涉及:秘书岗位相关的所有接待工作、电话业务、办公室事务、处理内外关系、人力资源相关事务、会议安排、差旅准备、宴请客户、参加展会、产品营销、公司财务等业务知识。每单元的内容选取和体例设置,均围绕创新型人才能力培养展开。

本教材内容结构分为以下几部分:

Listening Tasks

Section One

与单元主题相关的简单对话,在其中蕴含待人接物的礼仪。设置这部分内容旨在为后面的听说练习热身,对话语言浅显,确保每位学生(即使英语基础不好)都能听得懂,同时为接下来的听力理解和口语练习打下基础。

Section Two

与单元主题紧扣的听力文章,设置为有10个空缺的完形填空题,作为精听导入,培养和锻炼秘书的职业技能。练习设置充分体现秘书职业技能要求,涵盖了经常碰到的问题与处理方法,使基础知识与能力提高相互关照,关注每位学生的发展。

Section Three

听力篇章理解。该部分紧扣章节主题,以秘书在特定工作场景下的活动为主导内容,并结合跨文化背景,使学生深入听,仔细辨别,理解篇章的同时学习了解涉外秘书的职业特点及行业要求。练习的配备充分考虑到职业技能的锻炼和归纳概括能力的培养。

Oral Tasks

口语分 Pair Work 和 Group Work 两部分。Pair Work 部分以设定的情景对话为主,Group Work 部分以小组讨论为主。两部分的练习配置围绕单元主题展开,以 Listening Tasks 的内容为引擎,以商务活动和涉外秘书工作内容为背景,深入探讨商务礼仪和文化差异的处理方法,并对整章内容进行归纳总结,以口头的形式进行汇报练习。

本教程中听说部分内容丰富,练习量大,对课堂注意力的高度集中有很高的要求。因此,为活跃课堂气氛、激发学生的学习兴趣、开阔视野,本教程为教师提供了一些与单元内容有关的视频,专供课余学习和练习使用。

参与本教程筹划和编写的人员,多为来自高校的一线骨干教师,部分参编者还是双师型教师,曾在公司任职,有着丰富的实际操作经验和公司企业管理经验,还有来自一线岗位的外企涉外秘书人员。

涉外秘书专业教材的编写,还在不断的探索中,我们大胆地迈出第一步。在探索中前进,肯定会有这样那样的不足,万望同仁和专家提出批评和指正。

编　者
2013 年 2 月

Contents

Unit 1

You're welcome

Listening Tasks

Section One　Warming-up Exercises

Vocabulary

. . . .

Dialogue 1

| recognize | v. 认出,识别出 |

Dialogue 2

appointment	n. 约定,约会
available	a. 可与之交谈的
scheduled	a. 排定的,预定的

Dialogue 3

estimate	vt. 评估,评价
estimator	n. 评价师,评估员
refer	v. 委托
claim	v. 要求,索取

1

simplify   *v.* 简化

Dialogue 1

· ·

Fill in the blanks with the words or sentences you hear in Dialogue 1.

A: *Ms. Zhang* (*secretary*)   *B*: *Sales Manager*   *C*: *Joe Martin* (*customer*)

A: Sir, you called me?

B: Yes, Would you go to the airport and 1) _____ Mr. Martin?

A: Yes, with pleasure. When will he arrive?

B: He is arriving at 2) _____, but I think you should go there a bit earlier and make sure

3) _____.

A: Of course. I will carry a piece of paper with me. 4) _____.

B: Nice thoughts!

A: And shall I use the office car or taxi to drive him here?

B: Use the office car.

(*At the airport*)

A: Excuse me. But are you Mr. Martin from England?

C: Yes. I am Joe Martin. You must be Zhang Yao from Beijing ABC Business Company.

A: Yes. Nice to meet you, Mr. Martin.

C: Nice to meet you too, Ms. Zhang.

A: 5) _____.

C: No, thanks. I can manage it.

A: Did you have a good flight, Mr. Martin?

C: Wonderful! 6) _____. But how long will 7) _____?

A: About 45 minutes' ride. Our car is waiting over there. Let's go.

Dialogue 2

· ·

Listen to Dialogue 2 and then check the following statements. Write T for True and F for False in the brackets.

(   ) **1.** Mr. John Morris has an appointment with Ms. Xu.

(   ) **2.** The receptionist doesn't know the purpose of Mr. Morris' visit at first.

(   ) **3.** Ms. Xu is attending a conference outside the company.

(   ) **4.** The receptionist reports the visit to Ms. Xu.

(   ) **5.** The receptionist makes an appointment for Mr. Morris to meet Ms. Xu.

(   ) **6.** Mr. Morris will visit Ms. Xu next week.

Dialogue 3

Listen to Dialogue 3 and then answer the following questions.

1. What does the customer do?

2. Who referred him to come here?

3. Is the customer free today?

4. How does the receptionist help the customer?

Section Two   Cloze

Listen to a passage and fill in the blanks with the words you hear in the passage.

In 1870 Sir Isaac Pitman founded a school where students could 1) _____ as shorthand writers to "professional and commercial men." 2) _____ , this school was only for male students.

In the 1880s, 3) _____ , more women began to enter the field, and since World War I, the role of secretary has been primarily 4) _____ . By the 1930s, fewer men were entering the field of secretaries.

In an effort to 5) _____ professionalism amongst United States secretaries, the National Secretaries Association was created in 1942. Today, this organization is known as the International Association of Administrative Professionals (IAAP). The organization developed 6) _____ called the Certified Professional Secretaries Examination (CPS). It was first administered in 1951.

In 1952, Mary Barrett, president of the National Secretaries Association, C. King Woodbridge, president of Dictaphone Corporation, and American businessman Harry F. Klemfuss created a special Secretary's Day holiday, 7) _____ . The holiday caught on, and 8) _____ it is now celebrated in offices all over the world. It has been renamed "Administrative Professional's Week" to 9) _____

_____ , and to avoid embarrassment to those who believe that "secretary" refers only to women or to unskilled workers.

Section Three Listening for Details

Part A An interview

His First Rule of Business: Don't Hope

*This is an interview with **Ben Lerer**, co-founder and CEO of the Thrillist Media Group, which oversees men's lifestyle and shopping web sites.*

Vocabulary

. . . .

preach	*v.* 说教,劝诫
rely on	依靠
dedicated	*a.* 专注的,献身的
entrepreneur	*n.* 企业家,主办人
humiliate	*v.* 羞辱,使丢脸
spreadsheet	*n.* 电子数据表
inferior	*a.* 低等的,劣等的,次的
immature	*a.* 不成熟的

Exercise 1

Listen to the interview and put the following events in the order according to Mr. Lerer's experiences.

☐ **A.** When my best wasn't good enough, I was told I was very stupid.

☐ **B.** I didn't have confidence in what I was doing.

☐ **C.** I want to create a better situation for myself.

☐ **D.** I was young and immature and just got out of college.

☐ **E.** I was publicly humiliated by the manager.

☐ **F.** I don't want to be in a situation like this again.

☐ **G.** I really try to do that.

☐ **H.** I think we succeed more than we fail on a person-by-person basis.

Exercise 2

Listen to the interview again and then answer the following questions.

1. What does Ben Lerer mean by the expression "don't hope"?

2. When does a person usually feel regretted according to Mr. Ben Lerer?

3. When was the expression "don't hope" first used by Mr. Ben Lerer?

4. Why did he decide to leave his previous job?

5. How did he feel when he was mistreated by a manager?

Part B   Passage listening

Passage 1

Vocabulary

optical fiber	光纤
in lieu of	代替
private branch exchange（PBX）	专用分组交换机
customize	v．定制，定做
virtual	a．实际的，实质的；（计）虚拟的
utilize	v．利用，使用
mount	v．配有，安装
eliminate	v．消除，淘汰
office automation	办公自动化
adept	a．巧妙的，擅长于……的 n．专家，能手
courtesy	n．有礼貌的举止；谦恭有礼
attendant	n．服务人员

Exercise

Listen to the passage and choose the best answer from the four choices.

1. The live remote receptionist can do the following except _____.

    A. flexible call routing   B. order taking

    C. conference holding   D. customized greetings

2. New types of virtual video receptionist systems allow for live，in-house or remote locations to _____.

_____ .

A．manage office lobby areas from remote locations

B．call back phones

C．meet walk-in visitors

D．track visitors

3. The video receptionist can manage _____ office lobby areas.

　A．one　　　　　　　　　　　　B．many

　C．the whole building　　　　　D．none

4. The video receptionist is located _____ .

　A．at the gate of a building　　　B．at home

　C．far away from the office　　　D．in a central location

5. A skillful receptionist _____ in the business world.

　A．has been replaced by new technologies　B．will be abandoned

　C．is still very much in demand　　　D．usually has a very good image

Passage 2

Vocabulary

effective	*a*. 有效的
excel	*v*. 擅长,优于
iceberg	*n*. 冰山
etiquette	*n*. 礼仪,礼节
necessity	*n*. 必需品
multitask	*n*. 多任务;*v*. 使多任务
simultaneously	*adv*. 同时地
empathy	*n*. 同感,共鸣
groom	*v*. 梳洗
confidential	*a*. 机密的,秘密的
reputation	*n*. 名气,名声
gossip	*n*. 流言,闲话
professionalism	*n*. 职业特征,职业行为
hectic	*a*. 繁忙的,忙乱的
poker face	一本正经的面容,面无表情的人
hunt and peck	(美口)看着键盘打字

6

| knack | *n.* 窍门,技巧;本事,才能 |
| blab | *v.* 泄露秘密,瞎说乱讲 |

Exercise 1

Listen to the passage and tick（√）the skills and qualities mentioned in the passage.

☐ **1.** Education

☐ **2.** Blood type

☐ **3.** Ability to multitask

☐ **4.** People skills

☐ **5.** Hobbies

☐ **6.** Well groomed

☐ **7.** Strengths and weaknesses

☐ **8.** Ability to be discreet

☐ **9.** Computer and typing skills

☐ **10.** Reading speed

☐ **11.** Organizational skills

☐ **12.** Writing skills

☐ **13.** Work well under pressure

Exercise 2

Listen to the passage again and then answer the following questions.

1. What does "multitask" mean in this passage?

2. Why does the speaker say "If you are annoyed by people，then you will not make a good receptionist"?

3. Why is it important for a receptionist to pay attention to his or her appearance?

4. How can a receptionist avoid gossip matters?

5. Why are computer and typing skills important in a receptionist's work?

6. What specific work do receptionists usually organize?

7. Among all the skills mentioned by the speaker what kinds of skills do you have as a receptionist?

Oral Tasks

Section A   Pair Work

Task one: You are Janet Zhang. Your partner is Mr. Tom Lee, a client visiting your office. What can you say in the following conversation? Communicate the ideas and then change roles with your partner.

Task two: Work in pairs to match the opening small talk questions about travel, accommodation, and the weather (1 – 10) with the most appropriate response (A – J). Then practice with your partner.

1. What was the weather like when you left?

2. How do you find the weather here?

3. I suppose this weather must be a bit of a shock to you.

4. How was your trip?

5. Did you have any trouble finding us?

6. Did you get in on time?

7. How's the hotel?

8. Did you find somewhere to stay?

9. Have you got a room with a view?

10. Which hotel are you staying in?

A. Just a little bit late.

B. Pretty cold. It was only four degrees when I left home.

C. Not yet. Could you recommend somewhere?

D. No problem at all. The map you sent me was excellent.

E. I'm staying in the Lucky Hotel.

F. It is a bit. It was below zero back in the UK.

G. Lovely. Sunny skies. Nice and warm.

H. Unfortunately not. All I can see is the factory opposite.

I. Very comfortable, thank you.

J. Fine. Everything went smoothly, thank you.

1. _____   2. _____   3. _____   4. _____   5. _____

6. _____ 7. _____ 8. _____ 9. _____ 10. _____

✎ Section B Group Work

Task one: Work in groups of four to make a presentation on *How to Be a Good Receptionist*. You may follow the steps given as reference.

Step 1. Dress appropriately.

Step 2. Have phone numbers handy.

Step 3. Be courteous.

Step 4. Have a positive attitude.

Step 5. If someone is still being unreasonable, find a way to diffuse the situation.

Step 6. Give good directions.

Step 7. Keep busy.

Step 8. As soon as someone enters the office, direct your attention to him/her immediately, and give him/her a pleasant greeting.

Step 9. Answer the phone politely with a standard greeting such as "Good morning. Thank you for calling our company. My name is _____. How may I direct your call?"

Step 10. For visitors who come to the front desk, greet them with a smile and a standard greeting such as "Hello".

Step 11. Greet delivery personnel with the same professionalism and politeness as any other visitor.

Step 12. As an employee, if the boss asks you to do anything extraordinary, politely agree.

Task two: Every office that presents itself to the public in any way requires a face to meet the public. Although excellent communications over the phone and by email are important to the reception staff, it is the face-to-face communication that distinguishes a receptionist from a Customer Service Representative. Oftentimes, when a person (vendor, applicant, community member) enters your workplace, the first thing they will see is the receptionist — and first impressions are always important.

Discuss with you partners and tick (✓) what you think are proper behaviors and actions when you are at your office as a receptionist.

☐ **1.** Be nice to managers, see if you can help them with additional tasks during your free time.

☐ **2.** Find someone to take the desk for bathroom breaks, meetings, holidays, lunches, etc.

This way you avoid having angry people waiting for you when you return.

- [ ] **3.** Handling mail is usually part of a reception job, find out where it goes, who will bring it, and when, on your first day.

- [ ] **4.** You may be asked to perform other duties as well such as entering specific data, dispersing faxes or stuffing envelopes or a whole host of other duties depending on the size of your organization and the nature of the business.

- [ ] **5.** Remember to always have a pleasing attitude and to smile.

- [ ] **6.** Keep personal business away from your area — this includes cell phone calls and emails. IT departments can and will screen computer activities.

- [ ] **7.** Ask co-workers if they need help with anything. Better to make friends by helping than enemies by complaining.

- [ ] **8.** Remember what your role is at all times. You may be the first point of contact from people outside of your company or organization.

- [ ] **9.** Remember who signs your paycheck and respect them at all times.

- [ ] **10.** Always be willing to learn a new task or do a mundane task. Versatility goes a long way.

- [ ] **11.** You can be dismissive when you meet somebody you don't like.

- [ ] **12.** You can show your warm-heartedness and know-it-all.

- [ ] **13.** Fake being nice can work because people cannot see right through it.

- [ ] **14.** Sometimes complain or let co-workers know you're bored.

- [ ] **15.** You can show your strengths by getting into an argument with a caller or visitor.

- [ ] **16.** Eat food at your desk when you are free at the office.

- [ ] **17.** Wear casual clothing to show your sense of freedom.

- [ ] **18.** Wear colorful cologne or perfume or makeup.

Unit 2

May I speak to ...

Background Information

The first impression anyone gets from you will be lasting. Your voice on the other end of a telephone line is that first impression. You need to conduct yourself in a professional manner when calling people for business purposes.

It is an important office skill to be able to give a good first impression, either in person or when answering the phone. This applies not only to secretaries and reception staff, but to everyone who works within a business, with the primary concern being making the caller feel appreciated and valued while listening carefully to what he/she has to say.

Listening Tasks

Section One　Warming-up Exercises

Vocabulary

Dialogue 1

account	*n*. 账户
database	*n*. 数据库
considerably	*ad*. 相当大(或多)地
supervisor	*n*. 监督者,管理者
inquiry number	问询电话

Dialogue 2

to catch a person's name	听清楚名字
to be engaged	忙于……

to hold the line	不挂断电话
shipment	*n.* 船运，水运；（从海路、陆路或空运的）一批货物
postpone	*vt.* 延期；推迟
to be delayed	耽误，延误

Dialogue 3

preliminary	*a.* 初步的，预备的
consultancy	*n.* 顾问（工作）
venue	*n.* 会场
double-check	*v.* 复核
reserve	*v.* 预定，保留

Dialogue 1

· ·

Fill in the blanks with the words or sentences you hear in Dialogue 1.

R：Receptionist   C：Caller

R：Good afternoon，Northwest Electricity. Can I help you?

C：Good afternoon，this is Robert Tips. I have a question about 1) _____ .

R：I'd be happy to help you with that Mr. Tips. 2) _____?

C：I'm afraid I don't have that with me.

R：It's no problem. 3) _____ .

C：Great.

R：Could you give me your address as well?

C：4) _____ .

R：Yes，I have your account up on my computer. How may I help you?

C：The last bill I received seemed too high.

R：Yes，I see that it was considerably higher than last year. Did you use more electricity?

C：No，I don't think 5) _____ .

R：OK，I'll tell you what I can do. I'll 6) _____ .

C：Thank you. When can I expect an answer?

R：7) _____ . I'll give you an inquiry number.

C：OK，let me get a pen . . . . OK，I'm ready.

R：It's 3471.

C: That's 3471.

R: Yes, that's correct.

C: Thank you for your help.

Dialogue 2

· ·

Fill in the blanks with the information you hear in Dialogue 2.

1. Caller:_____

2. From:_____

3. To:_____

4. Telephone Number:_____

5. About: _____

6. Message: 1) _____

          2) _____

Dialogue 3

· ·

Listen to Dialogue 3 and choose the best answer from the four choices.

1. Mary Martin is calling from _____ .

    A. TAB Consultancy   B. TAB Consultancy & Promotions

    C. TEB Company   D. THB Company Ltd.

2. Mary Martin is calling about _____ .

    A. the order   B. the budget

    C. the trade fair   D. the conference time

3. Mary Martin has done some _____ .

    A. preliminary planning for the trip   B. preliminary work for the conference

    C. preliminary planning for the trade fair   D. preliminary trip for the meeting

4. The two things she likes to go over with Paul Smith are _____ .

    A. the hotel and the trade fair   B. the hotel and the reception

    C. the restaurant and the trip   D. the restaurant and the driver

5. The venue for the reception is at _____ .

    A. Plaza Hotel   B. airport

    C. railway station   D. Caesar's Restaurant

Section Two   Cloze

Choose the best words or expressions to complete the passage. Use the information you've just heard.

The most popular means of communication in the 21st century is text messaging. SMS, which __1__ short message service, is slow to enter, and you can __2__ key in 160 characters. The first text message was in 1992, but texting only became commercially available in 1995. In 1999 the number of texts sent __3__ one billion, and over the next three years, it grew to 20 billion. It __4__ part of youth culture. Some people don't use their mobiles to speak to people, only to __5__ friends, making arrangements and getting information __6__ 20 times a day. Companies are using texting for advertising and promotion. __7__ texting a special number, people can get a two-for-the-price-of-one discount for cinema tickets on Wednesdays, __8__ cinema attendance is the lowest. __9__ , cinema attendance has risen by nearly ten per cent. TV also uses text message voting. Texting has become one of the __10__ inventions for years.

1. A. symbolizes   B. stands for   C. identifies   D. stands out for
2. A. merely   B. but   C. only   D. only just
3. A. obtained   B. got   C. reached to   D. reached
4. A. quickly becomes   B. has quickly become
   C. has become quickly   D. becomes quickly
5. A. text   B. message   C. call   D. meet
6. A. as far as   B. until   C. up to   D. up until
7. A. By   B. Through   C. With   D. By means
8. A. which   B. when is   C. when is which   D. which is when
9. A. As a result   B. In the end   C. So that   D. Effectively
10. A. most leading   B. most successful C. more successful   D. successful

Section Three   Listening for Details

Part A   Choosing an appropriate voicemail message

Vocabulary

· ·

voicemail   *n*. 语音留言

timidity	n. 腼腆
professionalism	n. 职业化
take ... for granted	认为理所当然
achieve	v. 达到,取得
priority	n. 优先权
maturity	n. 成熟
read off	读出
concise	a. 简洁的
monotone	n. 单一的语调
ambient	a. 周围的,环境的
mumble	v. 咕哝

Exercise

Listen to the passage *Choosing an Appropriate Voicemail Message* and write down the five tips given in the passage.

1. Tip One：_____.

2. Tip Two：_____.

3. Tip Three：_____.

4. Tip Four：_____.

5. Tip Five：_____.

Part B   Passage listening

Passage 1

Vocabulary

effective	a. 有效的
remind	v. 使想起,提醒
humble	vt. 使谦恭

Exercise 1

Listen to the passage and tick（✓）the reasons causing difficulties in understanding people on the phone.

☐ 1. People are impatient.

☐ **2.** People speak too quickly.

☐ **3.** People on the phone are impolite.

☐ **4.** There are technical problems with the telephones.

☐ **5.** You can't see the person you are speaking with.

☐ **6.** It's difficult for people to repeat information.

Exercise 2

Listen to the passage again and then answer the following questions.

1. If some one speaks too quickly，what should we do?

2. When taking a note，what do we usually do on the phone?

3. What's the best way to solve the problem that you don't understand what the person said on the phone?

4. What can you attempt to do when the person on the phone couldn't slow down?

5. On what kind of situation can you begin speaking a different language on the phone?

Passage 2

· ·

Vocabulary

prospective	*a*．预期的；未来的；可能的
memorable	*n*．值得注意的事
utilize	*vt*．利用，使用
initial	*a*．起初的，开始的
interaction	*n*．配合，相互作用
converse	*v*．谈话
rapport	*n*．融洽，和谐；融洽的关系
convince	*v*．使相信；使明白
upbeat	*a*．积极乐观的
alert	*a*．机灵的，敏捷的 *v*．使注意
commonality	*n*．公共，平民
at ease	安逸，自由自在
lengthy	*a*．漫长的，啰嗦的
phone tag	互相给对方电话留言
persuasive	*a*．能说服的，善于游说的

16

lasting	a. 持久的, 恒久的
undivided	a. 专一的, 专心的, 全部的
distract	vt. 分散（注意力）

Exercise 1

Listen to the passage and tick（✓）the topics mentioned in this passage.

☐ 1. Greetings on the phone

☐ 2. Establishing a rapport

☐ 3. Message taking

☐ 4. Placing calls on hold

☐ 5. Asking questions with good manners

☐ 6. Ending a phone call with persuasive language

☐ 7. Alert

Exercise 2

Listen to the passage again and fill in the blanks with the information you hear in the passage.

1. Your first interaction by phone could mean _____. The initial conversation can _____.

2. Do not answer the phone while you are _____. _____ can all be detected over the phone.

3. In event planning, the goal of a conversation is _____. If you can establish a rapport over the telephone, _____.

4. It is important to _____. It will leave your caller with a lasting impression. Additionally, _____ will leave your caller looking forward to your next conversation.

5. _____ — it is not polite. Tell the client you will call him back when you can give him your undivided attention.

Oral Tasks

Section A Pair Work

Task one: Choose the best answer from the three choices.

1. You are in a restaurant with friends. Your mobile phone rings. You _____ .

    A. have a loud, long conversation on your mobile, ignoring your friends

    B. take the call and ask if you can call back later

    C. disconnect without answering

2. When you are watching a movie/play, you _____ .

    A. switch off your phone

    B. refuse to put the phone on silence/vibration mode

    C. set your phone on silence/vibration mode (step outside the movie hall/theater if the call is super-urgent or wait until the interval to call back)

3. You are taking a flight. A pre-flight announcement requests that all mobile phones be switched off until the plane lands. You _____ .

    A. wait until the plane comes to rest and you've disembarked before you switch on your phone

    B. think the instruction is a drag (negative or depressing)

    C. switch on the phone as soon as the plane begins to land

4. When you are driving, your cell phone rings. You _____ .

    A. check to see if a cop is watching before you take the call

    B. park at the side of the road and take the call

    C. take the call with your hands-free attachment

5. You're in a crowded place when your phone rings. You _____ .

    A. chatter away, ignoring the irritated stares

    B. take the call, speak in a voice lower than normal and decide the urgency

    C. refuse to take the call until you have some privacy

6. You are in an area where the connectivity is not good. Your phone rings. You _____ .

    A. disconnect and SMS (Short Message Service) that you'll get in touch later. And don't forget to get in touch

    B. take the call, speak in a loud voice to make sense of the interrupted conversation

    C. disconnect if the conversation is not clear. They can call back later

Task two: Discuss with your partner.

If the callers on the phone don't seem to be able to state their questions clearly and briefly, what should you do?

Section B Group Work

Task one: Discuss the following manners concerning phone calls with your groupmates and decide whether they are true or false.

1. When I'm with a business associate (生意客户), my cell phone rings and it's quite natural to answer it.

2. Always leave important phone calls to a landline. Cell phones are for casual and personal talks only.

3. Cell phones are convenient. It is appropriate to take a cell phone call wherever and whenever, including driving and playing golf, in public places and over business lunch. That's what cell phones are for.

4. My cell phone rings at a meeting. I know it's emergency. But for the sake of cell phone etiquette, just let it go.

5. It's appropriate and convenient to make business negotiations using text messaging.

Task two: Here are two examples on *How to Professionally Put a Caller on Hold*, read them and then discuss what you should do and what you shouldn't do when you are going to put a caller on hold.

"Mr. Smith, can you please hold while I retrieve your file?" {pause for a response} "Thank you. I will be back in a minute." {caller on hold} "Thank you for holding, Mr. Smith. I can now help you ..."

"Ms. Jones, I will check to see if Mr. Johnson is available to take your call. Can you please hold for a minute?" {pause for a response} "Thank you. I will be right back." {caller on hold} "I'm sorry for the inconvenience. Mr. Johnson is not available right now. May I have him call you back?"

Unit 3

The paper will be ready in a minute

Background Information

    A secretary is a person whose work consists of supporting management，including executives，using a variety of project management，communication and organizational skills. These functions may be entirely carried out to assist one other employee or may be for the benefit of more than one. In other situations a secretary is an officer of a society or organization who deals with correspondence，admits new members and organizes official meetings and events.

Listening Tasks

📖 Section One   Warming-up Exercises

Vocabulary

Dialogue 1

file-keeping	*n*. 文件整理，文件归档

Dialogue 2

blur	*v*. 弄脏，使……模糊
toner cartridge	硒鼓

Dialogue 3

delivery date	交付日期
deadline	*n*. 截止日期，最后期限
anyway	*ad*. 无论如何，不管怎样

Dialogue 1

Fill in the blanks with the words you hear in Dialogue 1.

A: President   B: Secretary

A: Would you please 1) _____ for me?

B: OK, I'll list down all the documents.

A: Remember this: The rule of file-keeping is "2) _____".

B: I'll get to work on it at once.

A: Have you found those files I 3) _____ yesterday?

B: Yes, I've found the files for you to examine. Here they are.

A: Thank you. And 4) _____ for today?

B: You have to meet the manager at 10 o'clock, and there is a meeting at 3 o'clock in the afternoon.

A: En ... please 5) _____ to next Tuesday at 2:00 pm.

B: You did say next Tuesday at 2:00 pm, didn't you?

A: Yes.

B: I understand. Do you have 6) _____ for this?

A: No. By the way, but you are going to have to re-do this planning.

B: I know. I'll get those plans over to your office by Friday.

Dialogue 2

Listen to Dialogue 2 and then check the following statements. Write T for True and F for False in the brackets.

(   ) **1.** The secretary said everything that came in the office fax machine last night is on the manager's desk.

(   ) **2.** The manager asked the secretary not to refax these copies.

(   ) **3.** The secretary will change the toner cartridge.

(   ) **4.** There are only 2 pages of these copies missing.

(   ) **5.** It looks like the fax machine is out of paper.

Dialogue 3

. . . .

Listen to Dialogue 3 and then answer the following questions.

1. What are they talking about?

2. What a discount did they promise to give?

3. Did they originally agree to a deadline in June?

4. When is the deadline?

Section Two Cloze

Listen to a passage and fill in the blanks with the words you hear in the passage.

As a business secretary, you need to be able to operate at your desk 1) _____ and easily. Though setting up a filing system sounds difficult, it is a relatively easy task that can be made easier by a few filing tips and tricks.

(1) Sit at your desk for a few minutes and 2) _____ where you will instinctively look for things.

I have a drawer to the right of my workstation. When I first set up my filing system, I didn't have anything in it. When I would look for stamps, paperclips or my stapler, it was the first place I would look, 3) _____ I knew it was empty. So naturally I put the stamps, paperclips and stapler in that drawer. For me, it was the natural home for those items.

Everyone will 4) _____ this differently, and what works for me may not work for you. Take a few minutes to sit down at your primary workspace and reach for equipment, supplies and files. That will help you establish the ideal spot for filing those items for you personally.

(2) Now that you know where you will naturally look for information, you must determine whether an alphabetical, numerical or subject filing system will work best for you.

Do you search for things according to the client's name? The category (i. e. expenses, financial, marketing)? By reference number? This is a 5) _____ step, as it will determine how you will lay out your filing system. Do this before you buy anything for your filing system.

(3) Next, roughly determine your storage needs.

Do you have a large number of files that you access 6) _____? Do you only access your files weekly? The answers will determine if you need a desktop file holder, a two drawer filing cabinet close to your desk or a four drawer lateral filing cabinet across the room. So many options exist today that you should choose carefully. Allow for growth when 7) _____ —

buy something to accommodate twice the files you think you will have now. This will limit the number of times you will have to resort and reorganize your filing system.

（4）Invest in a good labelling system for clarity and easy access.

Being able to read the file labels sounds obvious, but 8) _____ than you can imagine. Most companies who make labels provide templates that integrate with the most popular word processing software. You may want to consider one of the small label making systems that can now also print out individual mailing labels. Items that perform double duties are usually a wise investment.

（5）Now you are ready to purchase file folders.

The best investment I have found is to 9) _____ (make sure the plastic label tabs are included) and plain manila file folders for my filing system. I use colored hanging folders for two reasons：（1）easily available and （2）ease of recognition for categories. For example, all my client files are in yellow hanging folders, blue folders contain financial information and red is for marketing. This way, I can see roughly where I should be searching for a particular file.

The KISS principle 10) _____ that is easy to use and easy to grow with. Keep It Simple and Sweetheart! Broad subject categories will allow you to easily add new files as you grow, and will eliminate the need to upgrade or reorganize your filing system on a regular basis.

 Section Three   Listening for Details

Part A   Office regulations

Vocabulary

. . . .

decline   *n*. 下降,减少
slogan   *n*. 口号,标语
cumbersome   *a*. 笨重的,不方便的
confidentiality   *n*. 秘密,机密

Exercise 1

Listen to the passage and fill in the blanks with the correct sentences in the box.

Office Regulations

There has been a decline in personal standards of dress and conduct in the office recently.

The management will like to point out that all employees are expected to behave in a professional manner. We ask you to respect the following regulations:

1. Please dress tidily. _____ Men must always wear a jacket and tie. Pullovers and sweatshirts with advertising slogans on them are not acceptable.

2. Women should avoid wearing very high heels, especially the pointed kind. They make holes in the carpet and mark the wooden floors. _____

3. Please hang your coats up when you arrive. _____ This looks untidy and causes a bad impression.

4. Food packages would not be left on desks and tables. Empty containers would be put in the waste paper baskets. _____

5. Bottles and cans for soft drinks should be kept out of sight. _____

A. Please do not leave bottles or cans on desks.

B. Don't come to work in jeans.

C. Packets of biscuits would not be left on desks.

D. Recently we have noticed coats being hung over the back of chairs.

E. Please try not to wear them.

Exercise 2

Listen to the passage and fill in the blanks with the correct words in the box.

---

confusion; heading; regional; sequential; expansion

The terms Direct Access and Indirect Access related to filing systems explain the number of classification and whether the file can be accessed immediately or whether an index is needed.

Direct Access

This type of classification includes the following:

1. Alphabetical classification (the basis of most system)

It is simple and inexpensive to operate and most people can follow it easily. Its disadvantages are that it is cumbersome in a large system and _____ can arise with some names. Alphabetical rules must be followed consistently when filing by name.

2. Geographical classification

Files are arranged in alphabetical order according to the location of the topic or customer. This can be by country, region, town etc. It is useful where _____ information is required. It has the disadvantage of needing a certain amount of knowledge in order to be correctly used.

3. Subject

Files are given names according to the topic of their contents. The main subject _____ can be broken down into sub-topics which are filed alphabetically within the main topic. New sub-topics are inserted in sequence.

4. Indirect Access

Indirect access systems use some forms of numerical classification，usually sequential or in groups，in order to place information. Each document or folder is given a number and filed in order. Unlimited _____ is possible and it encourages accuracy. Confidentiality is easy to maintain.

5. It is essential to have an alphabetical index with any numerical system. This involves more work in setting up the system and maintaining it. Large numbers of files arranged in _____ number order become cumbersome unless strict control is maintained.

Part B   Passage listening

Passage 1

. . . .

Vocabulary

halo	n. 光环
perceive	vt. 注意到,觉察到
assertive	a. 坚定的，断定的

Exercise

Listen to the passage and choose the best answer from the four choices.

1. If you want to benefit from the so-called "halo-effect", you have to learn how to _____ .

   A. create a favorable impression   B. act as if you were playing cards

   C. dress   D. talk

2. When people meet you for the first time，they will _____ .

   A. judge you by your appearance and your manner

   B. listen to you patiently

   C. try to avoid eye-contact with you

   D. act as friendly as possible

3. What kind of person is likely to be accepted by the employer?

    A. One who is physically excellent.   B. One who is capable of talking.

    C. One who is fairly modest.   D. One who cares about oneself.

4. In the sentence "It's what's inside that counts." (Line 2，Para. 3), what does the word "count" mean?

    A. Do calculation.   B. Be important.

    C. Take into consideration.   D. Make a conclusion.

5. Which of the following could probably be the title of this passage?

    A. The Deepest Impression   B. Be More Confident

    C. The Attractive Four Minutes   D. How to Impress Interviewers

Passage 2

Vocabulary

facilitate	vt. 促进;帮助;使……容易
verification	n. 确认,查证

Exercise

Listen to the passage and then check the following sentences. Write T for True and F for False in the brackets.

(　　) 1. In this article，NZIS introduces the Student Bank Loan Scheme to facilitate easier processing of student visa applications from Chinese people who want to go to New Zealand.

(　　) 2. If the loan is approved，NZIS will then issue an 'Advice for Study Loan Abroad' document to the applicant or his or her parents.

(　　) 3. CIB requires deposits in the bank to be frozen and that they are at least 20% larger than the loan amount required.

(　　) 4. The applicant then lodges his or her visa application at the New Zealand Immigration Service (NZIS) together with the 'Advice for Study Loan Abroad' document.

(　　) 5. The applicant takes the notification from NAIS to the bank and completes a special application form to end the loan.

(　　) 6. The applicant submits this document，together with any other approval-in-principle requirements to CIB，who then finalizes the application.

Oral Tasks

Section A   Pair Work

Task one: Peter meets Diana, one of his colleagues, and consults her on where some office equipments are. What can they say in the following conversation? Communicate the ideas and then change roles with your partner.

Task two: Office equipment is essential in office automation, and secretaries may also use them in their daily life and work. As a secretary, you must be familiar with office equipment, so you will benefit from office automation. Below are some pictures of office equipment. Please give the English names of the following equipment, and discuss with your partner the functions of them orally.

1	2	3	4
5	6	7	8
9	10	11	12

Section B   Group Work

Task: Work in groups of four to make a presentation on *How to Make Business Travel Arrangements*. You may follow the steps given as reference.

Step 1. Discuss your travel needs with your supervisor, including the destination, the number of nights you expect to be away and the method of travel.

Step 2. Contact the person you will be meeting with to ask for the name of a nearby hotel.

Step 3. Obtain the name of the travel agent the company uses if you need to book your own travel.

Step 4. Ask the centralized booking resource for a detailed travel itinerary after the arrangements have been made.

Step 5. Contact the airline, hotel and rental car agency on your own at least a week before your trip to make sure the reservations are in place.

Step 6. Keep all of your receipts during your trip and be sure to fill out your expense report as soon as you return.

Unit 4

Please calm down

Background Information

Business Communication is any communication used to promote a product，service，or a company with the objective of making sale and getting profits. Business Communication can be of two types：oral communication and written communication.

Listening Tasks

Section One   Warming-up Exercises

Vocabulary

· ·

Dialogue 1

suggestion box	建议箱，意见箱
investigate	*vt*. 调查，研究
unrealistic	*a*. 不现实的,不切实际的

Dialogue 2

exhibition	*n*. 展览,展览会
arrangement	*n*. 安排
representative	*n*. 代表

Dialogue 3

oil refinery	炼油厂
seminar	*n*. 研讨会

Dialogue 1

Fill in the blanks with the words or sentences you hear in Dialogue 1.

(In the Marketing Department there is a "suggestions box" into which the staff from the department are encouraged to put their suggestions for improving efficiency. It is one of Tina's jobs to check the box and to report to Mr. Howard. Today, Tina has decided to look at the suggestions that have been made during the last month.)

T: Tina   H: Mr. Howard

T: Mr. Howard, are you busy?

H: 1) _____ , but what can I do for you?

T: I've just opened the suggestion box, and I wanted to have a word with you about some of the suggestions.

H: OK.

T: The first one is about 2) _____ . At present it's at 11:30.

H: Well, and what do you think?

T: I think we should have it a bit earlier, if that's OK.

H: 3) _____ .

T: Good. The second one is about 4) _____ .

H: Well, we can't replace it. But it might be a good idea to fit better cover so that it isn't so noisy.

T: OK, I'll investigate. The next one says "5) _____ ?"

H: A nice idea, but unfortunately unrealistic with so many people working in the same office. But why don't you talk 6) _____ to the office staff and see if the smokers can agree to smoke outside the office or something?

T: OK, I'll do that. That's all. Thanks very much.

Dialogue 2

Listen to Dialogue 2 and then check the following statements. Write T for True and F for False in the brackets.

(   ) 1. Mr. Tang will meet the boss at 9:30 in the morning.

(   ) 2. Miss Lin will call the boss at 10:30 in the morning.

(   ) 3. Only five representatives will take part in the conference.

(   ) 4. The boss will chair the conference.

(   ) 5. The conference focuses on the annual summary and new products' salses plan.

Dialogue 3

. . . .

Listen to Dialogue 3 and then answer the following questions.

1. Why does Ms. Zhang call to Mr. Jones?

2. What did Ms. Zhang arrange in Mr. Jones' schedule?

3. When is the field tour going to start?

4. Is there any change about the seminar?

Section Two Cloze

Listen to a passage and fill in the blanks with the words you hear in the passage.

A proper office manner should be 1) _____ by the secretary, and this manner should be based on the fact that the executive and the secretary are expected to work as a team. Whether working for an individual, a pair of executives, or a whole department, the secretary's duty is to 2) _____ the executive job responsibilities. Therefore, assignments that appear in the job description (if there is one) are done conscientiously, and those chores that do not appear but that need to be done in order to free the executive from routine tasks will be done by the professional secretary without grumbling.

As part of the team, the 3) _____ secretary protects the employer. He or she does not contribute information to office gossip but does report any rumor that may be helpful to the superior. Also, the professional does not spend company time on personal phone calls, in clock watching, or in being late.

The personal relationship between the executive and the secretary will vary according to the people involved and the 4) _____ of the company. The secretary should always remember that the relationship is a business arrangement and that the structure of any organization makes the executive more important than the secretary. Without the executive to 5) _____ and to plan for action to attain that objective, the secretary's job would not exist.

The executive may ask the secretary to explain a matter, but the secretary does not have the right to 6) _____ the executive to justify decisions. However, when a good working relationship exists, office authority is not a source of discontent because both the secretary and the executive realize that they are there to make that office run at 7) _____.

Personal life must be separated from professional life in dealing with all office personnel. It is very possible to work well with people one does not like at all; likewise, it is possible to work professionally with people who are personal friends. However, worries about sickness at home, financial problems, and 8) _____ do affect the quality of work, and the professional will do everything possible to keep the level of professional performance high.

In dealing with other members of the group, the secretary should make it clear that they are viewed as the experts in their jobs. The professional secretary is courteous to everyone 9) _____ _____ on the company ladder. The order-processing clerk, the shipping clerk, the receptionist, the typist, and the file clerk will be much more helpful to the secretary or executive team if this 10) _____.

 # Section Three　Listening for Details

Part A　IT managers

Vocabulary

. . . .

bachelor's degree　　　　　　　学士学位
replace　　　　　　　　　　　　*vt*. 取代,代替

Exercise

Listen to the passage and choose the best answer from the four choices.

1. Besides being the leader of computer technicians, IT managers are also expected to be _____.

   A. experienced product designers   B. skilled online technicians

   C. doctorate holders   D. online safety specialists

2. The word "reach" probably means _____.

   A. get in touch with   B. get to

   C. arrive at   D. meet the needs of

3. According to the passage, companies often look for IT managers from _____.

   A. non-computer technicians   B. their own professionals

   C. other companies   D. another country

4. Employers pay high salaries to IT managers because _____.

   A. they work hard

   B. they are excellent leaders

   C. they help improve the companies' products

   D. they are key factors to their success

5. The author of this passage intends to tell us _____.

   A. the important role IT managers play

   B. the advantages IT managers should have

   C. the qualifications IT managers possess

   D. the high salaries IT managers earn

Part B   Passage listening

Passage 1

Vocabulary

metropolitan   *a*. 大都市的

deployment   *n*. 部署,展开

Exercise

Listen to the passage and then check the following statements. Write T for True and F for False in the brackets.

(   ) 1. The company began by offering computer software solutions to local businesses in the greater Seattle metropolitan area.

(　) 2. The company was founded on an approach to providing simple communication solutions.

(　) 3. The company is expanding operations at the moment.

(　) 4. Global Call Communications employs more than 40,000 specialists.

(　) 5. The company expects to be servicing more than 50 million customers worldwide by 2005.

Passage 2

Vocabulary

equivalent　　　　　　　*a*. 等价的,相等的

Exercise

Listen to the passage and choose the best answer from the four choices.

1. The above is the _____ part of a job advertisement for a secretary.

   A. responsibilities　　　　　　B. qualifications

   C. application and screening procedures　　D. salary

2. Candidates must complete _____ .

   A. junior secondary education

   B. senior secondary education

   C. senior secondary education plus some specialized training in related areas

   D. vocational college education

3. All the following competencies are demanded EXCEPT _____ .

   A. basic computer skills　　　　B. English skills

   C. typing skills　　　　　　　D. excellent problem solving skills

4. Which of the following is mentioned in this passage? _____ .

   A. Where to file the application

   B. Holiday, sick leave and vacation benefits

   C. Mandatory retirement coverage with Public Employees Retirement System

   D. Typing or keyboard certificate

5. Which of the following is NOT true? _____ .

   A. There is no requirement in candidates' job experience in this field

   B. Candidates must be able to produce well-written English letters and reports

   C. They are looking for a bilingual secretary

D. People who to know little about computer are not qualified for this position

Oral Tasks

Section A　Pair Work

Task one：You are Sally. Your partner is Mr. Henson, a client visiting Beijing for the first time. What can you say in the following conversation? Communicate the ideas and then change roles with your partner.

Task two：You will stay in London on business for one week. Your secretary has contacted the following three hotels there. Discuss together which hotel you will stay at.

1. Royal London Hotel (five-star)
2. St. Steven's Hotel (three-star)
3. Hyde Park Gardens Hotel (four-star)

Section B　Group Work

Task：Work in groups of four to make a presentation on *How to Develop Effective Work Relationships*. You may follow the steps given as reference.

Step 1. Help other employees find their greatness.

Step 2. Keep your commitments.

Step 3. Bring suggested solutions with the problems to the meeting table.

Step 4. Your verbal and nonverbal communication matters.

Step 5. Share credit for accomplishments, ideas, and contributions.

Step 6. Never blindside a co-worker, boss, or reporting staff person.

Step 7. Don't ever play the blame game.

Unit 5

Congratulations on your promotion

Background Information

The secretary have some administrative duties and some opportunities to work directly with employers in company management. It is important for secretaries, especially administrative assistants, to be knowledgeable about management. Many secretaries assume supervisory duties over other office employees. They are responsible for not only choosing people with skills but also developing them into productive employees. In a word, an administrative secretary has the responsibility of recruiting, orienting, and training new employees.

Listening Tasks

Section One   Warming-up Exercises

Vocabulary

Dialogue 1

workload	n. 工作
replacement	n. 代替者
get stuck with	忙于;陷于

Dialogue 2

recruit	vt. 招募;招聘
be in one's shoes	处在某人的位置
shorthand	n. 速记
superior	n. 上级;上司

36

Dialogue 3

promotion	*n*. 升职
sentimental	*a*. 感情用事的;易伤感的
candidate	*n*. 候选人
know the ropes	掌握诀窍;知道内情
dynamic	*a*. 充满活力的;精力充沛的

Dialogue 1

Fill in the blanks with the words you hear in Dialogue 1.

Outlining the Job Requirements

A: Jason gave 1) _____ last week. We'll need to fill his position.

B: Oh no! My 2) _____ will double! How much notice did he give?

A: He gave two weeks. That gives us time to hire and train a 3) _____ .

B: More work!

A: No one will get stuck with more work if we quickly find a replacement! Now help me 4) _____ the requirements for a job ad.

B: OK. "Able to 5) _____ lunch, work 6) _____ , meet impossible 7) _____ ..."

A: No one will 8) _____ to that ad. Anyway, we'll require a four-year degree, preferable in marketing ...

B: Any experience!

A: We'll require two years experience. What else would you suggest?

B: The person needs to be 9) _____ , very 10) _____ , and able to work 11) _____ .

A: Right. You don't want to have to hold his or her hand all the time.

B: Exactly, that just means more work for me!

A: It won't be! Now, go and type up a job ad for me.

B: Ah-ha! Extra work already!

Dialogue 2

Fill in the blanks with the sentences you hear in Dialogue 2.

Recruiting New Staff

A: Well, I think you probably have a fair idea 1) _____ .

B: Yes, it was very clearly explained in the advertisement for applications.

A: Good. Perhaps you would tell me what sort of qualities you'd look for in your secretary

2) _____?

B: Well, to start with, I'd say she needs to be pretty hard-working.

A: Yes, as a matter of fact, I'm new to this job myself, but 3) _____

_____.

B: I've leant that the secretary of an export manager 4) _____.

A: Quite right. By the way, do you like travelling?

B: Oh, yes, especially abroad. And I speak French and German fairly fluently.

A: Excellent. Now I see from the report that 5) _____, and very

well indeed in the intelligence test. I suppose you'd be able to handle report writing,

summaries, keeping minutes at meetings and so on?

B: Yes, I've had to do quite a lot of that kind of work, and I seem to have a better memory than

average.

A: That sounds fine. By the way, 6) _____? We're a bit short of

space here as you can see.

B: From the secretary's point of view I think it's much better. 7) _____

_____.

A: Yes, I rather agree. Well, thank you very much, Miss Lu. And you'll be hearing from us in

the next few days.

B: Thank you, and 8) _____.

Dialogue 3

Fill in the form with the information you hear in Dialogue 3.

Committee member	John Jeffrys	Rita Hayden	Susan Palmer
Joan	_____ years With the firm Follower not _____	Shown _____ _____ _____	Too _____
Peter	_____	Too _____	_____ and _____
Clive	No experience of _____	Not ready _____ _____	A lot of _____

Section Two Cloze

Listen to a passage and fill in the blanks with the sentences you hear in the passage.

As a secretary, you should know the three distinct parts of the interview process:

Preparation before the interview

1) Be aware _____ .

2) _____ and then put it in newspapers and on your company's website.

3) _____ the persons qualified for your interview when applications come.

4) _____ and invite several qualified persons to run and sit in the interview.

5) _____ .

6) _____ .

The interview itself

7) _____ and regard the interview as both a selling and a matching process.

8) _____ .

9) _____ .

10) _____ .

11) _____ with the interviewee himself together, examine the interviewee fully.

12) _____ .

13) _____ .

Follow-up after the interview

After the interview, 14) _____ .

15) _____ and notefy the result of recruitment.

16) _____ for the position in the notification.

17) _____ and express best wishes in the notification.

 **Section Three**　Listening for Details

Part A　Company reorganization

Vocabulary

. . . .

feedback	*n*. 反馈
large-scale	*a*. 大规模的
compensation	*n*. 补偿；赔偿
drug test	药检
modify	*vt*. 改进；改善

Exercise

Listen to the dialogue and then answer the questions.

1. What is the basic aim of this reorganization according to the dialogue?

2. What is the policy for those qualified staff holding the positions that will be cut?

3. What is the policy for those who decide to quit?

4. What is their worry about this reorganization?

5. What is the benefit this reorganization will bring to the company?

Part B　Passage listening

Passage 1

. . . .

Vocabulary

seal the deal	成交
issue the invitation	发出邀请
gracious	*a*. 和善的；有礼貌的；大方的
reschedule	*vt*. 重新安排时间
grab	*vt*. 抓；抢；抢夺
quibble	*vt*. （对小的差别或分歧）争论
bashful	*a*. 害羞的；难为情的

boisterous   *a*.（指人或行为）喧闹的；活跃的

Exercise

Listen to the passage and choose the best answer from the four choices.

1. This passage is mainly about _____

   A. the importance of business meals.

   B. the selection of a good restaurant.

   C. seating arrangement.

   D. basic rules to make business meals pleasurable and profitable.

2. Which statement is not true according to the passage?

   A. Successful business meals are often well planned in advance.

   B. Proper seating arrangement can help make business meals pleasurable.

   C. If you attend to every detail in advance, things cannot go wrong.

   D. Hosts should try their best not to lost control in front of the guests.

3. Restaurants suitable for business meals are _____

   A. the ones you know well.   B. the ones where you are known.

   C. the latest hot spots.   D. both A and B.

4. Which of the following is NOT proper in seating arrangement?

   A. Work out the seating before your guests arrive.

   B. Make sure the guests have the best seats.

   C. Make your guests face the kitchen.

   D. If you have one client, sit next to each other.

5. Which of the following should be avoided for a business meal host?

   A. Changing the date at will.

   B. Quibbling with the restaurant over the bill.

   C. Complaining about the food and service of the restaurant in front of the guest.

   D. All of the above.

6. Which of the following is NOT correct about bill payment?

   A. It's best if the guests pay the bill.

   B. It's best if the bill doesn't come to the table.

   C. If the restaurant won't accept advance payment, make sure you grab the bill first.

   D. Make arrangements with the restaurant to pay the bill prior to the dinner, if possible.

Passage 2

. . . .

Exercise

Listen to the passage and then check the following statements. Write T for True and F for False in the brackets.

(   ) 1. Before you begin to write up a job ad, you have to know clearly the requirements of the job vacancy.

(   ) 2. As a recruiting clerk, you have to examine the amount of skills or knowledge of the candidate carefully.

(   ) 3. A person's personality is not as important as experience or qualifications.

(   ) 4. If you are looking for someone who deals with your largest clients, an aggressive person is a good choice.

Oral Tasks

Section A   Pair Work

Task one: You applied for the vacancy for assistant to Sales Manager in ABC Company. HR supervisor is interviewing you now. You're talking about your educational and working experience, salary, working date and so on. Make up a dialogue under the above situation.

Task two: In our daily life, we often go to parties, conferences or celebrations of certain events where we are likely to meet new people. What should we say to them if we want to get to know them? How can we say it politely? And what should we say in response if we are approached by a stranger at a social gathering? Make up a dialogue with your partner under the situation: You and Lucy Chen, working in the HR department meet each other at the annual dinner of your company and you two get to know each other.

Section B   Group Work

Task one: To claim competence at work, a secretary should be able to select the most appropriate type and means of communication to use, highly efficient in the use of telephone, fax and e-mail at workplace, plan and prepare a wide range of business documentation, use written communication skills and skills in the use of technology to produce accurate, well-constructed documents which create and maintain the image the organization wishes to convey. Have a group discussion on what may be the criteria for a secretary's management of business.

Task two: Good telephone manners is regarded as one of the chief requirements for office staff, therefore, it is obvious that it is highly rated among a secretary's qualification. On the phone, the secretary relies solely on his/her speaking skills. The customer's perception of the secretary and his/her company is determined entirely by his/her voice and choice of words. Have a group discussion on the tips for a secretary to get the most out of telephone calls.

Unit 6

This is final call for the meeting registration

Background Information

The role of a secretary is one loaded with multiple responsibilities. Coordinating administrative aspects prior to a meeting and taking minutes during the meeting are two of the tasks that an efficient secretary is expected to have mastered. However, to effectively summarize what is said during a meeting and turn this into reader-friendly points, is a skill that often comes with time, trial and error.

Listening Tasks

 **Section One** Warming-up Exercise

Vocabulary

Dialogue 1

promotion	*n.* 促销;提升
accommodate	*vt.* 容纳
entitle	*vt.* 使有资格;使有权
minutes	*n.* 备忘录;会议记录

Dialogue 2

ventilation	*n.* 空气流通;通风设备
vibration	*n.* 震动;摆动
refreshment	*n.* 点心;茶点;提神物

Dialogue 3

draft	*n.* 草稿

submit	v. 提交；上交
memo	n. 备忘录
file	vt. 归档

Dialogue 1

. . . .

Fill in the blanks with the words you hear in Dialogue 1.

A：Mr. Anderson   B：Judy

A：Judy，we're going to hold a 1) _____ next Friday afternoon. Please make all the necessary preparations.

B：No problem. Could you tell me the 2) _____ of the conference?

A：It's an important conference on the 3) _____ of our newly-developed products.

B：Where would you like the conference to be held?

A：At the Marsha Hotel. We need a meeting room which can 4) _____ about 200 people. You'd better get it reserved.

B：I'll do it right away. Apart from all the department managers，who else should be invited?

A：All the 5) _____ in Marketing Department will attend the meeting, and here's a list of 6) _____ . Don't forget to invite Mr. Green. He's very good at marketing，and we need his advice. You should 7) _____ that those entitled to be present are properly informed.

B：OK，anything else?

A：All the necessary 8) _____ and the information relevant to the meeting should be available，preferably printed out and 9) _____ before the meeting. And you should go to the meeting，make notes and then type out the 10) _____ from the notes.

B：OK. Anything else?

A：No，thank you very much.

B：Fine，and I'll get them done right away.

Dialogue 2

. . . .

Fill in the blanks with the sentences you hear in Dialogue 2.

A: *Mr. Anderson*   B: *Judy*

B: Mr. Anderson, is there anything I can do for you?

A: Yes, 1) _____ . Please get their name cards ready

right away.

B: No problem.

A: Please check and make sure 2) _____ . And ensure a notice is

placed on the outside door stating "Meeting Progress".

B: All right. Anything else?

A: We'd also add a friendly note: 3) _____ . Oh, by the way, when

shall we have the refreshment break?

B: From 10:00 am to 10:30 am. 4) _____ .

A: Thank you.

B: My pleasure.

Dialogue 3

. . . .

Listen to Dialogue 3 and then answer the following questions.

1. Did Mr. Parker attend the meeting yesterday? And why?

2. What did Mr. Parker ask May to do?

3. What did May ask Mr. Parker to do?

4. What about the date for the next meeting?

✎ Section Two Cloze

Listen to a passage and fill in the blanks with the words you hear in the passage.

In modern business, meetings are becoming more and more important since the majority of decisions are made during meetings. A secretary should know how to arrange a meeting effectively.

1) _____ . She or he should 2) __

_____ before fixing the date of a meeting; 3) _____ for the meeting venue, the seats, and the use of services, e.g. laptops, microphones, etc.; moreover, 4) _____ including the venue, date, time, together with the agenda to all concerned.

5) _____ and make sure she or he knows who they are. 6) _____. Don't try to write down every single comment — just the main idea. Write down motions, the persons who made them, and the results of votes. 7) _____. 8) _____ _____ while everything is still fresh in your mind. The minutes should include not only 9) _____, 10) _____ (daily, weekly, monthly, annual, or special), and 11) _____, but also the time when the meeting began and ended. 12) _____. The minutes of the meeting should be distributed to all who attended, any invitees who did not attend, and anyone else affected by the discussion.

Section Three Listening for Details

Part A Role of the secretary in a successful meeting

Vocabulary

. . . .

assist	vt. 帮助;协助
load	n. 重担
clerical	a. 事务上的
bylaw	n. 附则;法规
general body	全体(与会人员)
director board	董事会
vigilant	a. 警戒的;警惕的
take the roll call	点名
circulate	vt. 传递
supervise	vt. 监督;管理
treasurer	n. 会计;出纳员
assets	n. 资产;有用的东西
custodian	n. 管理人;保管人
facilitator	n. 帮助者;推进者

Exercise

Listen to the passage and fill in the blanks with the information you hear in the passage.

The secretary can assist the chair in 1) _____ , 2) _____ and 3) _____ a meeting.

I. Roles of secretary before the meeting

Secretary should be very clear about 4) _____ and 5) _____

_____

II. Roles of secretary during the meeting

6) _____

7) _____

8) _____

9) _____

III. Roles of secretary after the meeting

10) _____

11) _____

12) _____

13) _____

Part B   Passage listening

Passage 1   Rules for Taking Minutes

Vocabulary

time consuming	耗费时间的
specify	*vt.* 详细说明;指定;阐述
motion	*n.* 提议;议案
adjourn	*v.* 使中止;使延期
margin	*n.* 页面空白
intact	*a.* 完好无缺的
stenographer	*n.* 速记员
pose	*vt.* 提出
extract	*vt.* 摘录

Exercise

Listen to the passage and then answer the following questions in your own words.

1. According to the passage, what kind of information should the minutes specify?

2. According to the passage, when and how will the minutes be considered official?

3. What should the secretary do if he or she wants to make some correction or addition to the minutes?

4. What should be done if the organization wants to publish the minutes for public viewing?

5. What kind of information should the minutes to be published include according to the passage?

Passage 2

. . . .

Vacabulary

paramount	*a*. 极为重要的
haggle	*vi*. 讨价还价
highlight	*vt*. 突出;使显著
prolonged	*a*. 延长的;拖延的
tactile	*a*. 有触觉的
aggressive	*a*. 侵略性的;好斗的
integral	*a*. 不可或缺的
lavish	*a*. 非常慷慨的;浪费的
reciprocate	*vt*. 互给;互换
impact	*vt*. 对……发生影响
close the deal	达成交易

Exercise

Listen to the passage and choose the best answer from the four choices.

1. According to the passage, which of the following is wrong?

   A. Negotiation skills are of great importance in business.

   B. In South America, southern Europe and the Middle East, being on time for a meeting does not carry too much importance.

   C. In some countries, meeting with a handshake is not appropriate between men and women.

   D. Giving expensive gifts is an integral part of business protocol in the U.S.

2. Who would NOT regard the strong and direct eye contact as a conveyance of confidence and

sincerity?

  A. The American.

  B. The Englishmen.

  C. The Japanese.

  D. The Northern European.

3. According to the context, what does "Western societies are very 'clock conscious'" mean?

  A. Western people love clocks very much.

  B. Western people know clocks very well.

  C. Western people attach great importance to time.

  D. Western people are usually not on time.

4. According to the passage, in which region do business people like to get close when talking with each other?

  A. Europe.

  B. South America.

  C. North America.

  D. Japan or China.

5. According to the passage, in which region would being late be taken as a disrespect?

  A. China.

  B. South America.

  C. Middle East.

  D. Southern Europe.

Oral Tasks

Section A   Pair Work

Task One: Make up a dialogue on the following situation: You are Lily Wang, secretary of Mr. Andrew. An annual meeting is to be held tomorrow. Mr. Andrew, the boss, comes to you to make sure that everything is ready for the meeting.

Task Two: Speak out with one or two sentence(s) in English to your partner, using the following words or phrases, and then your partner interprets them into Chinese.

1. prepare; larger; in case; unexpectedly

2. schedule; time length; reference

3. breakout session; beamers; high-quality; enough

4. room block; peak period; summit; secure

5. pick up; the airport; temp staff; VIP delegates; responsible for

 ## Section B Group Work

Task One: Meetings provide people with opportunities to exchange information. The secretary is involved in activities such as preparing and facilitating meetings. He /She is required to make all the meetings effective from preliminary preparation to follow-up duties. Have a group discussion on *How to Organize a Meeting Effectively*.

Task Two: No one wants to look silly or do the wrong thing at a new job. It is important to make the right impression from the first day. You will face new people; you will be in new place. It will be difficult to know what to do. Discuss with your group members on *How to Make it through the First Day at a New Job*.

Unit 7

When are you leaving for the business travel?

Background Information

    If you work as an administrative assistant, an executive assistant or in some other administrative support role, at some point you'll likely make travel arrangements for one or more executives. Most corporations have contracts with travel agencies that work with airlines and hotels on the corporations' behalf or the companies themselves have in-house travel services. Either way, you'll set up executive travel through the entity serving the company's travel needs.

    Travel arrangements can be tricky and frustrating, but if you follow some simple steps and keep some basic information in mind, you can take away those hair-pulling moments and make your business travel an effective one. Planning, research and following a simple plan can reward you with travel arrangements that will result in a near-perfect trip.

Listening Tasks

 ### Section One　Warming-up Exercises

Vocabulary

. . . .

Dialogue 1

reserve	*v.* 保留,预定
available	*a.* 有空的,有效的
multi-function	*n.* 多功能

Dialogue 2

| airsick | *a.* 晕机的 |

| scales | *n.* 台秤,磅秤 |
| boarding pass | 登机牌 |

Dialogue 3

inspection	*n.* 检查
contraband	*n.* 违禁品;走私品
styling mousse	护发定型乳剂
combustibles	*n.* (复)易燃物;可燃物
aviation	*n.* 航空,航空学
explosive	*n.* 爆炸物
corrosive	*n.* 腐蚀剂
confiscate	*v.* 没收,充公

Dialogue 1

Fill in the blanks with the words or sentences you hear in Dialogue 1.

A：*Receptionist*　　*B*：*Secretary*

A：Beijing Friendship Hotel，Information Desk. 1) _____?

B：Yes. I would like to 2) _____ for Mr. and Mrs. Smith from Germany.

A：When will they come?

B：On October 20th.

A：How long will they stay?

B：For five days.

A：Just a moment，please，sir. I have to see whether any room is 3) _____. Yes，we can provide them with a room from October 20th to 24th.

B：Thank you.

A：By the way，may I know their 4) _____ in case the plane is late?

B：Sure. The flight number is CZ808 from Berlin to Beijing.

A：Thank you，sir.

B：Oh，one more thing. According to the program，Mr. Smith will give us a lecture on the 22nd. Could you arrange 5) _____?

A：Yes，sir. We have a 6) _____. We can arrange for you on that day.

B：Great. Thank you very much.

A: You're welcome.

Dialogue 2

. . . .

Fill in the blanks with the information you hear in Dialogue 2.

1. Seat: _____

2. Pieces of luggage to check: _____

3. Luggage weight: _____

4. Luggage allowance: _____

5. Excessive luggage charge: _____

6. Boarding gate: _____

7. Boarding time: _____

Dialogue 3

. . . .

Listen to Dialogue 3 and then answer the following questions.

1. What does the man ask the woman to put into the basket?

2. Why does the man stop the woman for inspection?

3. What kind of metal thing does the woman have on her?

4. What does she have in her hand luggage that is contraband?

5. Can she take it on board the airplane? Why?

6. How does the man solve the problem?

Section Two   Cloze

Listen to a passage and fill in the blanks with the words you hear in the passage.

Good afternoon, ladies and gentlemen. 1) _____ of China International Airlines Flight 2308 from Shanghai to New York. We wish you 2) _____ _____. The 3) _____ of this flight is 2:30 p.m. and the 4) _____ is 6:30 a.m. local time. The whole journey will be 16 hours, covering about 15,000 kilometers. It's now 2:20 Beijing time. The plane is going to 5) _____ _____ in 10 minutes. Would you please 6) _____ and fasten your seatbelts? Thank you. Ladies and gentlemen, if you look at the card in your seat pocket, you'll find where the 7) _____ are. In case of an emergency, 8) _____ will come down from overhead. Let me show you how to put it on. For over-water emergencies, we've 9) _____ under your seat. Please take it out and put it on in case of emergency. In addition, please 10) _____ _____ your mobile phone and stop using your electronic appliances such as 11) _____ _____ and CD players. Any use of electronic appliances may interfere with the electronic equipment of the plane. For the safety of all passengers, please 12) _____ _____. Thank you.

Section Three   Listening for Details

Part A   How to make travel arrangements for your boss

Vocabulary

snag	*n.* 阻碍
accomplish	*v.* 达到(目的),完成(任务),实现(计划)
accommodate	*v.* 容纳;向……提供住处;使适应,顺应
aisle	*n.* 过道,通道
preference	*n.* 偏爱,优先(权);偏爱的事物(或人)
shuttle service	班车服务
registration	*n.* 登记(证);挂号

| itinerary | *n*. 行程表,旅行路线 |
| precaution | *n*. 预防,防备,警惕 |

Exercise 1

Listen to the passage and tick（✓）the instructions mentioned in the passage.

☐ 1. Find out what kind of transportation he prefers.

☐ 2. Book a ticket when everything is settled.

☐ 3. Use the frequent flyer number while booking a flight.

☐ 4. There is no need to ask your boss if you know his or her preference.

☐ 5. Buy some food if your boss needs a quick meal during the trip.

☐ 6. Print out maps if your boss plans to drive.

☐ 7. List the restaurants or coffee shops nearby the hotel.

☐ 8. Confirm all reservations the day before the trip.

Exercise 2

Listen to the passage again and then answer the following questions.

1. What does the speaker mean by the expression "hit some snags"?

2. Before you buy the flight ticket，what should you do?

3. What should you inform the hotel clerk if you have selected a hotel?

4. What should you do if your boss plans to drive?

5. How to make a travel itinerary?

Part B Passage listening

Passage 1

Vocabulary

jet lag	飞行时差反应
nuisance	*n*. 令人讨厌的人（东西或行为等）
digestive	*a*. 消化的,易消化的
internal	*a*. 内的,内部的
adjustment	*n*. 调整

Exercise

Listen to the passage and choose the best answer from the four choices.

1. What is the problem a person suffers from when traveling between time zones?

    A. Adjusting his biological clock.

    B. Knowing the direction of a jet.

    C. Realizing the time difference during flight.

    D. Getting used to the weather of a new place.

2. For how many percent of people, it is a real problem?

    A. 49.　　　　B. 54.　　　　C. 45.　　　　D. 55.

3. How many hours does one need to get over his jet lag problem if he travels across three zones?

    A. 24.　　　　B. 36.　　　　C. 48.　　　　D. 72.

4. What's the main purpose of the passage?

    A. To explain the cause of jet lag problems.

    B. To teach us how to avoid jet lag problems.

    C. To explain the differences between time zones.

    D. To show the ways to arrange time properly.

5. According to the passage, which journey causes fewer problems?

    A. A west-to-east journey.

    B. An east-to-west journey.

    C. A north-to-south journey.

    D. A south-to-north journey.

Passage 2

. . . .

Vocabulary

executive	*a*. 行政的
routine	*n*. 例行公事
vehicle	*n*. 交通工具,车辆
desired	*a*. 要求的,想要的
confirmation	*n*. 证实
itinerary	*n*. 行程表
clarify	*v*. 澄清,阐明
identical	*a*. 同样的,相等的

Exercise 1

Listen to the passage and tick (✓) the information points mentioned in the passage.

☐ 1. Hotel preference

☐ 2. Dress preference

☐ 3. Transportation preference

☐ 4. Travel agent preference

☐ 5. Date and time of departure desired

☐ 6. Type of restaurant desired

☐ 7. Class of accommodations desired

☐ 8. Any special needs

☐ 9. Flight number

☐ 10. Bank account

Exercise 2

Listen to the passage again and then answer the following questions.

1. What information should the secretary give the hotel or travel agent when making a hotel reservation?

2. When speaking directly to someone at the hotel, what should the secretary get?

3. When making airline reservation, why is it important to get the name of the person involved?

4. What should the secretary do when some guests visit the company?

5. What is the main idea of this passage?

Oral Tasks

Section A Pair Work

Task one: You are Mr. /Miss Wang. Your partner is a receptionist of China International Airlines. You are going to book an open return ticket to New York for next Monday on Flight 308. But this flight has booked up. What can you say? Try to make up a conversation, then communicate the ideas and change roles with your partner.

Task two: Work in pairs to match the opening small talk questions (1-9) with their responses (A-

D). Then practice with your partner.

1. Good evening! China Hotel! Can I help you?

2. What price would you like to pay per night, sir?

3. Mr. Hamilton, how long do you intend to stay?

4. May I have your ID card? And how are you paying the bill?

5. I wonder if it's possible to reserve a small conference room in your hotel for the 20th?

6. I wonder how long does the laundry service take?

7. Is there a fitness room in the hotel?

8. Can I use them free?

9. Here is the key, sir. This way, please.

A. Yes, here you are! I'll pay by credit card.

B. Yes, we have a conference room which holds about 15 people.

C. I think I'd better have a moderately priced room.

D. Yes, and a swimming pool, sauna and tennis courts.

E. Good evening! I'd like to book a double room with a bath.

F. Yes, it's included in the price.

G. All right, thank you very much!

H. I'll stay here for three nights from May 14th to 16th.

I. Laundry is collected at nine in the morning and will be returned on the afternoon of the same day. It takes about 8 hours.

1. _____ 2. _____ 3. _____ 4. _____ 5. _____

6. _____ 7. _____ 8. _____ 9. _____

Section B Group Work

Task one: Work in groups of four to make a presentation on *How to Prepare a Business Trip*. You may follow the steps given as reference.

Step 1: Set goals.

Step 2: Set up appointments.

Step 3: Send information ahead.

Step 4: Pack essential items.

Step 5: Update contacts.

Task two: Whether this will be your first or your thousandth business trip, you should be conscious of conduct that is considered proper during your absence from the office. As a representative of your company, you need to know how to behave appropriately on a business trip. Discuss with you partners and make a presentation on *How to Behave Appropriately on a Business Trip* according to the following instructions. Pay attention to the tips and warnings.

Instructions

☐ Pack all essential items in a carry-on bag to avoid being ill-prepared for business in case that the airline loses your luggage.

☐ Dress professionally during the entire trip.

☐ Be prepared and be on time.

☐ Use proper business language.

☐ Brush up on table manners and the basics of business etiquette before you go.

☐ Save all receipts from your trip so you can easily determine your expenses when you return.

☐ Conduct yourself with grace and decorum at all times.

Tips

☆ Ask if you can smoke before lighting up.

☆ Use a personal phone card to make long-distance phone calls while you are away.

☆ Before you leave, make sure to buy a guidebook or consult someone who has recently traveled to your intended destination to learn about the culture and customs.

☆ Find someone to take care of the table for bathroom breaks, meetings, holidays, lunches, etc. This way you avoid having angry people waiting for you when you return.

Warnings

◇ Avoid planning leisure-time activities during your trip if they will detract from the amount of business you are able to conduct.

◇ Stay away from pornography, alcohol and anything potentially inappropriate during your trip.

◇ Keep in mind that your time is not your own on a business trip.

Unit 8

Let's drink to our friendship

Background Information

    The ability to entertain clients is one of the best skills to have in any corporate setting. If you impress your clients, it means repeated business and other perks down the road. The trick to entertaining clients is to find out what they enjoy doing and make sure that they have a good time while in your company. With some preparation, you can have a lot of fun entertaining clients. Does this spark an idea?

Listening Tasks

Section One   Warming-up Exercises

Vocabulary

. . . .

Dialogue 1

splendid	*a*.（口语）极好的；绝妙的
catering culture	饮食文化
cuisine	*n*. 烹饪（风味）
assorted	*a*. 各种各样的,混杂的,什锦的
saute	*v*. 煎,炒（食物）
toffee apples	拔丝苹果

Dialogue 2

dessert	*n*. 餐后甜点
stuffed	*a*. 吃饱了
raspberry	*n*.（植）覆盆子,树莓

Dialogue 3

sumptuous	*a*. 奢侈的
flexible	*a*. 灵活的，可变通的
propose	*v*. 提议，建议（某事物）
toast	*n*. 祝酒辞
negotiation	*n*. 协商

Dialogue 1

Fill in the blanks with the words or sentences you hear in Dialogue 1.

A：*Mr．Wang*（*a Chinese businessman*） *B*：*Mr．Smith*（*a foreign customer*）

A：What about going out for a meal this evening, Mr. Smith?

B：That's very kind of you, Mr. Wang. I hear Chinese restaurants 1) _____．

A：Yes, China is a country with a splendid 2) _____．

（At a Chinese restaurant）

A：Mr. Smith, I wonder if you have any 3) _____．

B：Oh，as the saying goes，"4) _____．" I only want to taste real Chinese food.

A：This is a Beijing restaurant，5) _____． I suggest we start with a plate of assorted cold dishes as an appetizer，then shrimps sautéed with green peas，steamed turtle，followed by Beijing roast duck，fried noodles，and toffee apples for dessert.

B：That sounds fabulous! Let's have that.

A：Would you like to try some Chinese drinks?

B：Yes，I'd love to. I've heard Maotai is very popular in China. Could we try some?

A：Yes, of course. Maotai is the best Chinese wine. It would be a pity 6) _____．

Dialogue 2

Listen to Dialogue 2 and then check the following statements. Write T for True and F for False in the brackets.

(   ) 1. Tim would not like any dessert because he wants to have more delicious dish.

(   ) 2. Helen wants some dessert because she thinks the food is excellent.

(   ) 3. Tim doesn't seem to be full enough.

(   ) 4. Tim would like to have some coffee because he wants to keep awake.

(   ) 5. Elizabeth will drink some hot tea, too.

Dialogue 3

Listen to Dialogue 3 and then answer the following questions.

1. What kind of meal do they have?

2. Is Mr. Lin's company very busy? Why?

3. What approach in foreign trade does Chinese government adopt?

4. What does Mr. Lin say to Mr. Bowen in order to express his hospitality?

5. What toasts do they have to each other at the banquet?

Section Two Cloze

Listen to a passage and fill in the blanks with the words you hear in the passage.

How much time should I spend entertaining my customers? Good question. The world of the field salesperson is changing 1) _____ these days, and everything is in question. The practice of entertaining customers is one of those 2) _____ that needs to be rethought.

Consider this experience of mine. I had a 3) _____ account that did not respond to my efforts. 4) _____ went by, and I could get nowhere in this huge account. My company 5) _____ four season tickets to the University of Michigan football games, and it was my turn to use them. I invited the head of the 6) _____ department from that account and her spouse to join my wife and I. We spent the afternoon together, first enjoying a 7) _____ tail-gate meal, then a great college football game.

Immediately thereafter, however, 8) _____. Business grew continually until it eventually became my largest account. 9) _____ in the relationship. It wasn't that I gained "inside" information. We didn't even talk about business. But, my customer came to know me better, and, in doing so, 10) _____ _____ . And that made all the difference.

Section Three   Listening for Details

Part A   Entertaining clients over meals

Vocabulary

. . . .

essentially	*ad*. 本质上,基本上
knowledgeable	*a*. 有丰富知识的,博学的
setting	*n*. 环境,背景
demonstrate	*v*. 论证;说明;显示
accomplish	*v*. 达到(目的),完成(任务),实现(计划)
prime	*a*. 首要的;最好的
specialty	*n*. 特产,名产,特色菜
savvy	*n*. 常识;理解

Exercise 1

Listen to a passage and tick（✓）the things that you should do when entertaining your clients over food.

☐ **1.** Be patient at business meetings.

☐ **2.** Be knowledgeable about the product you are dealing with.

☐ **3.** Go to unfamiliar places for the new atmosphere.

☐ **4.** Arrive on time.

☐ **5.** Be creative.

☐ **6.** Take your time.

☐ **7.** Be thoughtful when choosing a restaurant.

☐ **8.** Let your guest be seated where he or she can see the outside view.

☐ **9.** Show good conversational skills.

☐ **10.** Start business discussion when all the guests are seated.

Exercise 2

Listen to the passage again and then answer the following questions.

1. Why does the speaker say that business meals are business meetings essentially?

2. When should you invite your client for breakfast?

3. What should you do if you are late for dinner?

4. How to make suggestions when it comes to ordering food?

5. When to begin the business discussion?

Part B   Passage listening

Passage 1

. . . .

Vocabulary

business contacts	生意上的熟人
atmosphere	*n.* 气氛
disadvantage	*n.* 劣势,弊端
tough	*a.* 困难的
colleague	*n.* 同事

Exercise

Listen to the passage and choose the best answer from the four choices.

1. According to the passage，why do people like to see clients away from the office?

　A. To know their business partner better.　　B. To enjoy the dishes only.

　C. To have a relaxation.　　D. To escape from the company.

2. When people see two men having dinner together from their office，what do they think?

　A. It must be something unusual.　　B. It's a business appointment.

　C. It's a hot debate on their life.　　D. It's a private talk.

3. According to the passage，what do men usually prefer to do with other men?

　A. Playing tennis.　　B. Shopping.

　C. Dancing.　　D. Drinking.

4. How to solve the problem if a woman dines with male clients?

　A. Go to a private house.　　B. Take another colleague.

　C. Take one's husband or wife.　　D. Leave it alone.

5. Why does the author dine with male-clients in places likely to be seen by her colleagues?

　A. Because they would admire her for having so many clients.

　B. Because she doesn't want to dine far from the office.

C. Because she doesn't care what people think of her.

D. Because they would believe she is doing business.

Passage 2

Vocabulary

slouch	*v*. 低头垂肩地站（或坐，走）
masticated	*a*. 嚼碎的
slurp	*v*. 饮食出声
corollary	*n*. 必然结果
unappetizing	*a*. 引不起食欲的，引不起兴趣的
leisurely	*a*. 悠闲的，从容的
digestion	*n*. 消化
forearm	*n*. 前臂
mashed potatoes	土豆泥
courtesy	*n*. 有礼貌的举止或言行
smudge	*v*. 涂脏　　*n*. 污点
napkin	*n*. 餐巾

Exercise 1

Listen to the passage and put the following basic table manners in the right order according to the speaker.

☐ A. Keep your elbows off the table.

☐ B. Don't reach.

☐ C. Don't speak with your mouth full of food.

☐ D. Excuse yourself when leaving the table.

☐ E. Sit up straight.

☐ F. Wipe your mouth before drinking.

☐ G. Compliment the cook.

☐ H. Eat at a leisurely pace.

☐ I. Don't forget "Please" and "Thank you".

☐ J. Chew quietly, and try not to slurp.

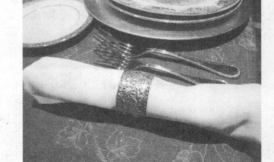

Exercise 2

Listen to the passage again and then answer the following questions.

1. Why are good table manners so important?

2. What should you do if you feel you must speak immediately during the dinner?

3. Why should we eat at a leisurely pace?

4. Why should we keep our elbows off the table?

5. What should you do if you must leave the table?

6. How to compliment the cook if the food is awful?

Oral Tasks

Section A Pair Work

Task one: Suppose you want to invite your friend, Mr. White, to lunch tomorrow. But he has already made an arrangement for that day. So make it the day after tomorrow. Make up a dialogue with your partner and then change your roles.

The following points are given for your reference.

1. Point out the time you want to meet.

2. Point out Mr. White's arrangement tomorrow.

3. Mention the restaurant.

4. Mention the place you are going to meet.

Task two: Work in pairs to match the opening small talk questions about dinner (1-8) with the most appropriate response (A-H). Then practice with your partner.

1. George, how about having dinner with us tonight?

2. I'll meet you at the entrance of the hotel at six tomorrow evening. Is that OK?

3. May I propose a toast to brisk business and continuing development?

4. May I have the bill, please?

5. Waitress, can I pay with a traveler's check?

6. Miss, what's this amount for?

7. Sir, may I take a print of your card?

8. Please put it on my bill.

A. I'm afraid not. We can only accept cash.

B. Certainly, here you are.

C. It's the service charge.

D. Oh, how nice of you! I'll be very glad to come.

E. Certainly sir. Thank you.

F. Very well. I'll be waiting for you then.

G. Thanks. Here's to your health and success in business as well.

H. Just a moment. I'll get it ready for you.

1. _____ 2. _____ 3. _____ 4. _____

5. _____ 6. _____ 7. _____ 8. _____

Section B   Group Work

Task one: Work in groups of four to make a welcome speech. You may follow the steps given as reference.

Step 1. Understand the speech's purpose and how much time you have to deliver it.

Step 2. Greet the attendees at the beginning of the speech and welcome them to the event.

Step 3. Tell the attendees why they should be interested or excited to be at the event.

Step 4. Provide an overview of what will occur at the event.

Step 5. Introduce other speakers or key players in the event.

Step 6. Express hopes for the event and the attendees' enjoyment of it.

Step 7. Conclude by thanking the audience for attending.

Task two: Sometimes these dinners are dull and stuffy. Sometimes they are nights of drunken gluttony. No matter what type of business meeting you may be a part of, here are some rules to guide you across this tightrope of professional dining. Discuss with you partners and make a presentation on *How to Behave at a Business Dinner* according to the following instructions. Pay attention to the tips and warnings.

Instructions

☐ 1. Eat. The purpose of the dinner is to partake of a meal with colleagues of some sort.

☐ 2. Mind your manners.

☐ 3. Unless there is hesitation or confusion over who will order first, there is no need to blurt out your order. Take your turn.

☐ 4. Depending on your dinner guests, alcohol may be inappropriate, appropriate or expected.

☐ 5. Order a drink and pretend to sip at it or order something nonalcoholic if alcohol is expected and you do not drink.

☐ 6. Engage in harmless talk to get people warmed up if conversation is quiet, stilted or difficult to begin.

☐ 7. Keep your meal choice reasonable if you are not picking up the tab.

☐ 8. Let your colleagues know that it is okay to order the most expensive thing on the menu if you are paying for the meal.

☐ 9. Tell the waiter to bring you the check before the meal is over in the above situation.

☐ 10. Keep to the topics at hand if the dinner is to discuss business.

Tips

☆ If the peer pressure to drink is enormous, excuse yourself to the facilities and on the way ask your waiter to bring you a virgin cocktail (without announcing its virgin status). When you return from the facilities, you can casually mention that you caught the waiter and asked for a drink.

Warnings

◇ Unless it is expected that you drink to excess, be mindful of your alcohol intake. Remember, this remains business and you must be able to control your judgment.

Unit 9

This is our latest product

Background Information

How to effectively publicize the products of your company? Attending trade fairs or exhibitions, receiving visitors to your company or factory, making an impressive product introduction or presentation as well as implementing potent marketing strategies are all essential ways to make a publicity campaign. Also, companies have to develop good products and services, attract people by powerful product description and adopt various promotional tools to generate sales. In addition, marketing mix which contains the basic "4Ps" (product, place, price and promotion) requires much effort and consideration to propose a marketing plan before launching any product.

Listening Tasks

Section One Warming-up Exercises

Vocabulary

Dialogue 1

international trade show	国际贸易展
at present	现在,目前
light industrial product	轻工业产品

Dialogue 2

digital TV	数字电视
warranty	n. 保修(期)
reputation	n. 声誉,声望
transaction	n. 交易

| available | a. 有空的,可得到的,能与之交谈的 |

Dialogue 3

arthritis	n. 关节炎
launch	v. 发起,推出（新产品）
prescription	n. 处方,药方
over-the-counter	a. 不需要处方也可销售的
publicity campaign	宣传活动
leaflet	n. 传单

Dialogue 1

Fill in the blanks with the words or sentences you hear in Dialogue 1.

Mr. Zhou, a businessman from ABC Company Ltd, would like to get some information of this coming international trade show and a general idea of the exhibition hall.

Z: Mr. Zhou   R: Receptionist

R: Good Morning, sir. Can I help you?

Z: Good morning, I'm a representative of ABC Company Ltd. At present, 1) _____ _____. We plan to set up business relationships with foreign countries to 2) _____ _____. So we would like to get a general idea of your international trade show.

R: It's our pleasure to help you. The exhibition consists of 4 halls, including halls for 3) _____ _____, light industrial products, metals and chemical products. Visitors can see samples of what there is to buy. Many trade companies come here and 4) _____ _____. The exhibits are mainly of new products which have been produced by various factories. Which hall are you particularly interested in?

Z: I'm interested in the second one, light industrial products.

R: OK. We can go upstairs to the hall of light industrial products. By the way, you can 5) ____ _____ which contains the map for our exhibition hall and 6) _____.

More and updated information can be obtained on our website as well.

Z: That's good to know. Thank you very much for your assistance.

Dialogue 2

. . . .

Listen to Dialogue 2 and then check the following statements. Write T for True and F for False in the brackets.

(   ) **1.** The quality of this new digital TV series is better than other similar products.

(   ) **2.** These TVs look fashionable and are not equipped with remote controls.

(   ) **3.** The warranty on this TV is 2 years.

(   ) **4.** The company offers home service round the clock if something goes wrong with the product.

(   ) **5.** Mr. Andrew is also interested in the technology of the products as well.

(   ) **6.** The supervisor is available and happy to talk with Mr. Andrews now.

Dialogue 3

. . . .

Exercise 1

Listen to Dialogue 3 and then answer the following questions.

1. Who is Arthran for exactly?

2. Where is this drug going to be available?

3. What should doctors suggest when their patients take this drug? Why?

Exercise 2

Listen to Dialogue 3 and complete the table.

Marketing Process	Time
	end of April
visit doctors in hospitals and surgeries	
give posters to doctors	
	in five weeks' time — on 25 May

Section Two Cloze

Listen to a passage and fill in the blanks with the words you hear in the passage.

A Well-Planned Sales Presentation

A well-planned sales presentation provides the necessary organization of the salesperson's materials; in addition, it requires him or her to 1) _____ the products or service sales features and benefits that are appropriate in a particular sales situation. To ensure 2) _____, the salesperson must plan how to communicate the sales manager best.

Next, the salesperson must go over the material in order to breathe as much life and vigor as possible into the 3) _____. Sufficient impact must be created to cause the prospect to understand the message, believe the message, and remember the message. The message must be exciting and convincing enough to motivate the prospect to 4) _____. Webster's dictionary defines "dramatic" as "full of action, highly emotional; vivid, exciting, powerful, approached from the view point of drama". The series of activities designed to 5) _____ by the buyer is called dramatization.

Each salesperson is expected to 6) _____ into the sales presentation. No two people are likely to use exactly 7) _____ to put their message across. Salespeople should ask themselves the following questions: "How can I use my imagination and resource fullness to 8) _____?" "How can I use my abilities to make my presentation a little different and a little stronger?" Salespeople 9) _____ _____. They are always trying to do a better and more effective job of selling.

Section Three Listening for Details

Part A Promotion strategies

Promoting a new product

This interview with John Bass concerns the promotion strategies used in the launch of Fresh Fries, an updated machine for making fries.

Vocabulary

. . . .

bright   *a.* 明亮的

path	*n.* 小路、路径
location	*n.* 位置、地点
publicity	*n.* 宣传、宣扬
secondary	*a.* 次要的、从属的
confirm	*v.* 确认
novelty	*n.* 新颖、新奇
trial	*n.* 试用、试验

Exercise 1

Listen to the interview and tick （✓） the topics mentioned in the interview.

☐ **1.** Where the machines are situated

☐ **2.** Publicity in newspaper

☐ **3.** Publicity on television

☐ **4.** Giving away the fries for free for a trial period

☐ **5.** Letting the machine operators have a free trial

☐ **6.** Paid advertising

☐ **7.** The color of the machine

☐ **8.** The fact that this is a novel product

☐ **9.** The price of the machine

☐ **10.** The size and shape of the machine

☐ **11.** The unique taste of the product

Exercise 2

Listen to the interview again and then answer the following questions.

1. What will they do to ensure that people will notice their products?

2. What will they do to get free time on television?

3. What is the best advertising they can get according to the experts? And what are they going to do?

Part B   Passage listening

Passage 1

. . . .

Vocabulary

selling point   产品特色

74

briefly	*ad.* 简要地
version	*n.* 版本
timer	*n.* 计时器
dice	*n.* 骰子
magnetic	*a.* 有磁性的
retail	*n.* 零售价
discount	*n.* 折扣

Exercise

Listen to the passage and then check the following statements. Write T for True and F for False in the brackets.

(   ) **1.** There are more than two versions of the game called Mindtwist.

(   ) **2.** The travel version is lighter and smaller compared with the standard version.

(   ) **3.** The magnetic board of travel version measures just 23 cm square and the total weight is lighter than 300 grams.

(   ) **4.** The standard version sells cheaper than the travel version.

(   ) **5.** The company has simplified their game instructions for their customers.

Passage 2

. . . .

Vocabulary

attempt	*v.* 尝试、企图
technique	*n.* 技巧
analysis	*n.* 分析
reaction	*n.* 反应
appeal	*n.* 吸引
purchase	*n.* 购买
feature	*n.* 特点
feasibility	*n.* 可行性
package	*v.* 打包

Exercise 1

Listen to the passage and choose the best answer from the four choices.

1. Which of the following method is not included in the "survey" technique to seek information?

   A. Go to exhibition or shops.

   B. Telephone or visit a company.

   C. Interview or face-to-face talk with people.

   D. Analyze the data from the questionnaire.

2. When a new product is introduced to a limited area, a/an _____ is needed on customers' reactions to it.

   A. analysis　　　　B. observation　　C. note-taking　　　D. tape-videoing

3. Once the need for a certain type of product is established, research can show the most desired designs or _____ .

   A. locations　　　B. sizes　　　　　C. prices　　　　　D. features

4. The manager's job is to _____ .

   A. plan the market strategy

   B. learn and study the market information for the product

   C. supervise the sales activities

   D. establish a well-organized marketing system

5. According to the passage, which of the following is NOT a thing that a manager will consider?

   A. Purchase ability of other companies or people.

   B. Publicity and advertising.

   C. Packaging and shipping.

   D. The price of the new product.

Exercise 2

Listen to the passage again and then answer the following questions.

1. What is the intention of doing a market research?

2. What are the three techniques to obtain primary information in business?

3. Which technique is illustrated in the example of "selecting students to help decide the fashion style in the following season"?

4. What is the job of product research?

5. What does "market feasibility" mean?

Oral Tasks

Section A Pair Work

Task one: Work in pairs to match the questions involved in the product introduction and sales process (1 - 10) with the most appropriate answers (A - J). Then practice with your partner.

1. The quality sounds all right, but your price seems to be too high.
2. Can you briefly tell me the new features of your latest model?
3. Can you give me a few brochures that will further explain what you can offer?
4. Can you deliver the goods to our place?
5. Will it be guaranteed?
6. Is it a wholesale price?
7. I believe your goods are all far above standard quality.
8. Can you customize your product?
9. How about your after-sales service?
10. How do you control the quality?

A. Sure. I may refer you to the brochure you'll find all the specifications and prices of our different models.

B. Of course. We'll deliver the goods directly from the warehouse to your place when you have paid the full amount.

C. No, it is a retail price. If you order in large quantity, we will give you a preferential price.

D. In spite of the high price, it will compete well with existing brands. The design is more modern than any of the current rival products.

E. Thank you for saying that. Yes, we always put quality as the first consideration. We never sacrifice quality for quick profits.

F. Yes, we are happy to make any possible changes to the product to meet the specific needs of our customers.

G. All the products have to go through five checks during the manufacturing process.

H. We've attached great importance to our after-sales service and we are always glad to be of your service. So if you find there is something wrong with our products anytime and anyplace, please do not hesitate to call our free after-sales service number ...

I. Yes, it will be guaranteed for 2 years. During this period, we will offer free maintenance every three months for the machine.

J . Yes, we put this model on the market just two months ago. It has a smaller size and more convenient to carry. Besides it is easier to operate and consume less power. So it is a wise choice for English learners.

1. _____   2. _____   3. _____   4. _____   5. _____

6. _____   7. _____   8. _____   9. _____   10. _____

Task two: You are Jenny Wang and you are presenting your products in the Chinese Export Commodities Fair. Your partner is Mr. John Zhang, a client who is visiting your product show room. What can you say in the following conversation to get the product well publicized? Communicate the ideas and then change roles with your partner.

Prompts for conversation:

The product introduction may involve the shape, size, feature, benefits, unique selling propositions, quality and price of your product as well as a brief comment of your company.

Presenter:

☆ Our company deals with/produces/specializes in/provides (textile trade, furniture, chemicals, Information Technology ...)

☆ Our company has gained a renowned reputation in the market both home and abroad.

☆ We enjoy 40% of Chinese market and we are the largest ... provider in China.

☆ It is designed for ...

☆ They are different in many ways, it is more ...

☆ Our product is of superior quality and we are offering some discounts or a few models.

☆ The machine gives you an edge over your competitors.

☆ I think you will agree it is much better value for money.

Visitor:

☆ Your ... impressed me very much at the fair.

☆ The design is novel and appealing to eyes.

☆ Can you go over the new features you have added to the latest model?

☆ Can you give me a price list with specifications?

☆ We could consider making a deal with your company as long as ...

Section B   Group Work

Task one: Work in groups of four to make a speech on *How to Do a Good Presentation*. You may choose some suggestions from the following statements or add your own techniques after discussion. And then explain and specify what to do according to these suggestions.

☐ Consider your audiences.

☐ Prepare your talk.

☐ Make microsoft power point.

☐ Choose visuals aids to support the presentation.

☐ Practice your presentation.

☐ Preparation on scene.

☐ Good presentation manners.

Task two:

In the early 1960s, Professor Neil Borden at Harvard Business School identifies a number of company performance actions that can influence the customer decision to purchase goods or services. Borden suggested that all those actions of the company represented a "Marketing Mix". The marketing mix contained four elements: product, price, promotion and place. If you want to market a product successfully, you need to get this mix right.

In addition to the standard four "Ps", what other factors should be taken into consideration in terms of marketing? Discuss in groups and try to find more words starting with "P" (e. g. people, position, process) and then explain the standard and the extra "Ps" in your own words.

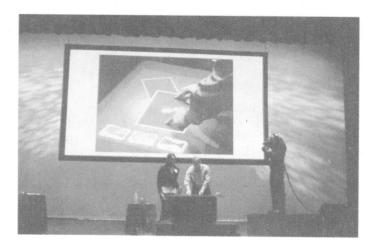

Unit 10

This is beyond our budget

Background Information

Budget is an estimate of costs, revenues, and resources over a specified period, reflecting a reading of future financial conditions and goals. As one of the most important administrative tools, a budget serves also as a (1) plan of action for achieving quantified objectives, (2) standard for measuring performance, and (3) device for coping with foreseeable adverse situations.

Listening Tasks

Section One   Warming-up Exercises

Vocabulary

Dialogue 1

itching	*a.* 渴望的
proceed	*vi.* 前进,进行
itinerary	*n.* 行程,旅程
receipt	*n.* (企业、银行等)收到的款,收据
reimburse	*vt.* 偿还;付还

Dialogue 2

loan	*n.* 借款
credit position	资信情况
joint venture	合资企业
commercial loans	商业贷款
currency	*n.* 货币;流通

adopt	v. 采用,采取
floating rate	n. 浮动汇率
Balance Sheet and Profit and Loss Statement	资产负债表

Dialogue 3

register	v. 登记,注册
enterprise	n. 企业,公司
real estate	房地产
constructive material	建材
authority	n. 官方,当局
be subject to	受支配,从属于……
value added tax	增值税
respectively	adv. 分别地
prescribed materials	规定的材料
approve	v. 批准,通过

Dialogue 1

Listen to Dialogue 1 and choose the best answer from the four choices.

1. Jean is going to her first business trip for _____.

    A. a trade fair   B. a marketing seminar

    C. sales promotion   D. a marketing research conference

2. Jean should get a corporate card because _____.

    A. there will be more business trips coming up

    B. she likes to use corporate card to pay her trip

    C. her boss asked her to do so

    D. the secretary asked her to do so

3. Jean can only use the corporate card for _____.

    A. hotels and meetings   B. transportation tickets

    C. food   D. air ticket

4. Jean should make sure to attach _____ to her expense account when she comes back to get her money reimbursed.

    A. business report   B. invoices   C. business itinerary D. receipts

Dialogue 2

. . . .

Fill in the blanks with the words or sentences you hear in Dialogue 2.

A: *Ms. Green*   B: *Mr. Smith*

A: Hi, good morning, Mr. Smith. How are you?

B: Good morning, Ms. Green. I'm fine, thank you. But I really need your help.

A: What can I do for you?

B: You know National Electrical Paris Shanghai Ltd. has been operating well since its establishment. But now we have a project for expanding, which is still 1) _____ _____. Could you 2) _____?

A: Well, as a regular customer 3) _____, and because a joint venture is a corporate body in China, you can meet the commercial loans terms of China. 4) _____ _____?

B: Canadian dollar. What about the interest rate?

A: 5) _____. The interest will be calculated at the floating rate published every day by the People's Bank of China. How much do you want to borrow?

B: 6) _____.

A: Generally speaking, there should be no problem. Anyway, I have to 7) _____ _____ again. Do you have them now?

B: Here you are.

A: OK. 8) _____.

B: Thank you very much.

Dialogue 3

. . . .

Listen to Dialogue 3 and choose the best answer from the four choices.

1. The company runs the businesses of _____.

    A. real estate development

    B. constructive material production

    C. real estate development & the sale of constructive material

    D. real estate development & the production of constructive material

2. The company should register _____.

    A. national tax authorities

B. regional tax authorities

C. either national tax authorities or regional tax authorities

D. A and B respectively

3. In the process of registration the company should get and fill in the application form, and _____ .

    A. present the prescribed materials   B. present the business certification

    C. present the business qualification   D. present business documents

4. The tax registration is due _____ after the company has received business certificate.

    A. 30 days   B. within 30 days   C. within 13 days   D. 13 days

5. The charge of the registration is _____ .

    A. 200 yuan   B. 100 yuan   C. 1,000 yuan   D. 2,000 yuan

 ## Section Two Cloze

Listen to a passage and fill in the blanks with the words you hear in the passage.

    Budget meetings are important because they allow you to present to your boss or superiors 1) _____ . In the meeting you can discuss possible increases or decreases 2) _____ and suggest ways to 3) _____ .
Budget meetings also allow you to 4) _____ for your project or work.
Overall budget meetings determine 5) _____ , and set goals and limits
for controlling the money and remaining profitable. It is relatively easy to set up a budget
meeting.

Section Three   Listening for Details

Part A   Creating a budget proposal

Vocabulary

· ·

budget proposal	预算提案
venture	*n.* 活动,(经济)行为
release	*v.* 释放
revenue	*n.* 收入
accountable	*a.* 可说明的,可解释的,负责人的
submit	*v.* 提交
incorporate	*v.* 合并
integrate	*v.* 成为一体,一致
spreadsheet	*n.* 电子数据表
plot	*v.* 制图
potential	*a.* 潜在的
incur	*v.* 引起,发生
duration	*n.* 持续,期间
highlight	*v.* 强调,突出
net revenue	净收入
subtract	*v.* 减
scrutiny	*n.* 仔细查看,监督

Exercise

Listen to the following passage and number the sentences in the order you hear.

☐ A. Plotting everything down on a spreadsheet will make it easier for your potential investors to read.

☐ B. When creating your budget,the first thing you should plot down is the projected expenses.

☐ C. A budget proposal is a realistic cost and revenue analysis that provides the path to a particular goal interpreted in numbers.

☐ D. Investors only care about the bottom line and realistic goals proposed.

☐ E. If you need to detail how you came to a particular amount, place notes or reference the numbers to the written explanation located in your overall proposal.

☐ F. If the return is good and realistic, then it will increase the chances of the project getting approved.

☐ G. Make sure that your numbers stand scrutiny. If possible, be conservative on the numbers to ensure that the funds will cover what the project needs.

☐ H. Once you are done with the expenses, list down all the potential revenue streams for the project.

☐ I. If your budget proposal is for a project to develop profit, then you will need to balance the budget.

Part B   Passage listening

Passage 1

. . . .

Vocabulary

executive	*n.*	主管,高级行政人员
relevant	*a.*	有关的
entry-level	*a.*	初级的
candidate	*n.*	候选人
agenda	*n.*	议事日程
address	*vt.*	向……讲话,发表演说
resolve	*v.*	解决(问题)
perspective	*n.*	想法,观点
primary	*a.*	首要的;主要的;基本的
operational	*a.*	操作的,经营的
input	*n.*	输入
floor	*n.*	发言权

Exercise 1

Listen to the passage and tick（√）the topics mentioned in the passage.

☐ 1. Methods of preparation

☐ 2. Choose Candidates

☐ 3. Review Meeting Guidelines

☐ 4. Follow an Agenda

☐ **5.** Set New Goals

☐ **6.** Listen to Input

☐ **7.** Close the budget meeting

Exercise 2

Listen to the passage again and then answer the following questions.

1. What candidates are usually included in the budget meetings?

2. Why should the guidelines or meeting rules be reviewed before the meeting starts?

3. What is usually included in the agenda?

4. What is the function of the agenda?

5. Why should the floor be open for other employees attending the meeting, when excutives may have the word for most of the addressed issues?

Passage 2

Vocabulary

derive	*v*. 源于
accurately	*adv*. 准确地
critical	*a*. 关键的,重要的
cater	*v*. 提供饮食及服务
quotation	*n*. 行情,报价
subcontractor	*n*. 转包商
portion	*n*. 一部分
mark-up	标价,标记
estimate	*v*. 估计,估价
rate sheet	收费表,价目表
billing rate	开单价
multiply	*v*. 增加,相乘
figure	*v*. 计算在内;估计
client	*n*. 委托人;顾客,常客
capital	*n*. 资本,资金
equation	*v*. 相等,平衡
wreck	*v*. 毁坏

culprit	*n.* 引起不良后果的人（或事物）
overage	*a.* 过老的；*n.* 过剩，过多
storage	*n.* 储藏

Exercise 1

Listen to the passage and fill in the blanks with the information you hear in the passage.

1. Project budgets are concerned with two things：_____.

2. List all items _____.

3. List all tasks _____.

4. Figure _____.

5. Look for hidden costs _____.

Exercise 2

Listen to the passage again and tick（✓）the true statements.

☐ 1. Cost is the amount that the customer will pay for the project.

☐ 2. Small costs including catering for meetings，travel costs to visit the project site and other items necessary，usually quickly add up on a big project.

☐ 3. Multiply the total number of hours for each person by the cost and bill rates to get the labor cost and price.

☐ 4. Most large companies have no standard cost-of-capital equation that can be used to figure the cost.

☐ 5. If a business must purchase product，or pay employees before it receives money from the client，then it will have to use its own capital to pay for these items.

☐ 6. All costs can be anticipated，so you don't necessarily go over your budget plan.

Oral Tasks

Section A   Pair Work

Task one：Work with your partner and get familiar with the following expressions relating to "money".

1.	bad money	无利可图的钱
2.	bank money	银行票据
3.	blood money	抚恤金
4.	boot money	企业赞助体育的钱
5.	call money	活期存款
6.	cheap money	低息借款
7.	dear money	高息借款
8.	dark money	加班费
9.	earnest money	定金
10.	fairy money	捡的钱
11.	folding money	纸币
12.	front money	预会金
13.	glove money	贿赂
14.	good money	有利可图的钱
15.	hard money	价格比较稳定的钱
16.	hot money	短期流动资金
17.	hush money	赌别人嘴的钱
18.	pill money	零花钱（pocket money｜pin money）
19.	push money	提成
20.	ready money	现金
21.	seed money	本钱，本金
22.	silly money	来路不明的钱
23.	smart money	有经验者（或知情者）投资的钱；了解内情的人
24.	table money	餐费
25.	tall money	大笔的财富
26.	trust money	委托金

Task two: Work with your partner and discuss the following questions.

1. Does the ability to manage money well come from experience, or does good advice count too?

2. How have credit cards changed people's attitude to money?

Section B Group Work

Task one: Work with your group and make a presentation on *How to Set a Budget Meeting*. The following suggestions may help you.

1. Determine who should attend the budget meeting.

2. Check the schedules of everyone you are inviting to the meeting.

3. Choose duration for the meeting, such as 30 or 60 minutes.

4. Pick a day and time for the meeting.

5. Send out a meeting request notification via email.

6. Reschedule the meeting if people who need to be there are unable to attend.

7. Remind all attendees about the upcoming meeting that week or that morning.

Task two: Work in a group. As treasurers of a university club, you are going to give the financial report to the club committee. Think about:

1. the type of club, for example, a debating club or a drama club;

2. the size of the club's budget, which depends on the number of members and the annual subscriptions;

3. the club's expenditure on, for example, guest speakers' meals and traveling expenses;

4. the cost of running expenses, for example, stationary expenses.

Income in RMB		Expenditure in RMB	
Subscriptions	2,600	Transport to events	2,634
University aid	2,000	Printing for leaflets	549
Alumni donation	2,500	Additional coaching	1,800
Sales of T-shirts	250	Performance videos	644
Sales of sports bags	295	Lectures on sports medicine	1,800
TOTAL	7,645		7,427

Bibliography

1. 新编剑桥商务英语教师用书(初级)2 版/(英)威廉斯(Williams, A.),(英)伍德(Wood, L.),(英)劳埃德—琼斯(Lloyd-Jones, C.)编著. — 北京:经济科学出版社,2002.3
   Pass Cambridge BEC Preliminary Teacher's Guide
   ISBN 7-5058-2938-6

2. 新剑桥商务英语(初级)教师用书/(英)琼斯—麦克齐奥拉(Jones-Macziola, S.)著. — 北京:人民邮电出版社,2004.8
   Further Ahead: Teacher's Guide by Sarah Jones-Macziola
   ISBN 0-521-59784-6
   Originally published by Cambridge University Press in 2002

3. 商务秘书实用英语/汤平平主编. — 北京:中国建材工业出版社,2004.8
   (21 世纪高等教育商务秘书系列教材)
   ISBN 7-80159-670-6

4. 新剑桥商务英语(高级)教师用书/(英)麦肯齐(MacKenzie, I.)著. — 北京:人民邮电出版社,2004.9
   English for Business Studies: Teacher's Book (Second Edition) by Ian MacKenzie
   ISBN 0-521-75286-8
   Originally published by Cambridge University Press in 2002

5. 外贸英语/宋德祥主编. — 南开:南开大学出版社,2004.10

6. 实用商务英语综合教程/ 沈素萍主编. — 北京:科学出版社,2009
   (大学英语选修课系列教材)
   ISBN 978-7-03-023606-7

7. 商务英语口语实力派/ 王慧莉,刘文宇,李强主编. — 大连:大连理工大学出版社,2011.5
   (赢在职场)
   ISBN 978-7-5611-6160-9

8. 商务英语/ 阮绩智,张彦主编. — 杭州:浙江大学出版社,2011.12
   ISBN 978-7-308-09379-8

9. 商务英语听说/ 孙宁,于晓言编著. — 北京:外语教学与研究出版社,2009

10. 商务英语听力教程(第二册)/ 刘亚珍,张丽主编. — 北京:北京理工大学出版社,2010

11. 商务交际英语听说/ 宋朝生主编. —— 广州:暨南大学出版社,2010

12. 国际商务英语会话/ 滕美荣主编. —— 北京:首都经济贸易大学出版社,2009

13. 商务英语口语/ 隋晓冰主编. —— 北京:机械工业出版社,2004

14. http://www.ehow.com/how_17591_behave-appropriately-business.html

15. http://www.ehow.com/how_1000325_behave-businees-dinner-url.html#ixzz2MTg5c2vB

Vocabulary

accommodate　v. 容纳;向……提供住处;使适应,顺应

accommodate　vt. 容纳

accomplish　v. 达到(目的),完成(任务),实现(计划)

accountable　a. 可说明的,可解释的,负责人的

account　n. 账户

accurately　adv. 准确地

achieve　v. 达到,取得

address　vt. 向……讲话,发表演说

adept　a. 巧妙的,擅长于……的　n. 专家,能手

adjourn　v. 使中止;使延期

adjustment　n. 调整

adopt　v. 采用,采取

agenda　n. 议事日程

airsick　a. 晕机的

aisle　n. 过道,通道

alert　a. 机灵的,敏捷的　v. 使注意

ambient　a. 周围的,环境的

analysis　n. 分析

anyway　ad. 无论如何,不管怎样

appeal　n. 吸引

appointment　n. 约定,约会

approve　v. 批准,通过

arrangement　n. 安排

arthritis　n. 关节炎

assertive　a. 坚定的,断定的

assets　n. 资产;有用的东西

assist　vt. 帮助;协助

assorted　a. 各种各样的,混杂的,什锦的

at ease　安逸,自由自在

at present　现在,目前

atmosphere　n. 气氛

attempt　v. 尝试、企图

attendant　n. 服务人员

authority　n. 官方,当局

available　a. 有空的,可得到的,能与之交谈的

aviation　n. 航空,航空学

bachelor's degree　学士学位

Balance Sheet and Profit and Loss Statement　资产负债表

bashful　a. 害羞的;难为情的

be in one's shoes　处在某人的位置

be subject to　受支配,从属于……

billing rate　开单价

blab　v. 泄露秘密,瞎说乱讲

blur　v. 弄脏,使……模糊

boarding pass　登机牌

boisterous　a. (指人或行为)喧闹的;活跃的

briefly　ad. 简要地

bright　a. 明亮的

budget proposal　预算提案

business contacts　生意上的熟人

bylaw　n. 附则;法规

candidate　n. 候选人

capital　n. 资本,资金

catering culture　饮食文化

cater　v. 提供饮食及服务

circulate　vt. 传递

claim　v. 要求,索取

clarify　v. 澄清,阐明

clerical　a. 事务上的,文书或办事员的

client　n. 委托人;顾客,常客

colleague　n. 同事

combustibles　n. (复)易燃物;可燃物

commercial loans　商业贷款

commonality　n. 公共,平民

compensation　n. 补偿;赔偿

concise　a. 简洁的

confidential　a. 机密的,秘密的

confidentiality　n. 秘密,机密

confirmation　n. 证实

confirm v. 确认

confiscate v. 没收, 充公

considerably ad. 相当大(或多)地

constructive material 建材

consultancy n. 顾问(工作)

contraband n. 违禁品; 走私品

converse v. 谈话

convince v. 使相信; 使明白

corollary n. 必然结果

corrosive n. 腐蚀剂

courtesy n. 有礼貌的举止或言行

credit position 资信情况

critical a. 关键的, 重要的

cuisine n. 烹饪(风味)

culprit n. 引起不良后果的人(或事物)

cumbersome a. 笨重的, 不方便的

currency n. 货币; 流通

custodian n. 管理人; 保管人

customize v. 定制, 定做

database n. 数据库

deadline n. 截止日期, 最后期限

decline n. 下降, 减少

dedicated a. 专注的, 献身的

delivery date 交付日期

demonstrate v. 论证; 说明; 显示

deployment n. 部署, 展开

derive v. 源于

desired a. 要求的, 想要的

dessert n. 餐后甜点

dice n. 骰子

digestion n. 消化

digestive a. 消化的, 易消化的

digital TV 数字电视

director board 董事会

disadvantage n. 劣势, 弊端

discount n. 折扣

distract vt. 分散(注意力)

double-check v. 复核

draft n. 草稿

drug test 药检

duration n. 持续, 期间

dynamic a. 充满活力的; 精力充沛的

effective a. 有效的

eliminate v. 消除, 淘汰

empathy n. 同感, 共鸣

enterprise n. 企业, 公司

entitle vt. 使有资格; 使有权

entrepreneur n. 企业家, 主办人

entry-level a. 初级的

equation v. 相等, 平衡

equivalent a. 等价的, 相等的

essentially ad. 本质上, 基本上

estimate v. 估计, 估价, 评估, 评价

estimator n. 评价师, 评估员

etiquette n. 礼仪, 礼节

excel v. 擅长, 优于

executive a. 行政的; n. 主管, 高级行政人员

exhibition n. 展览, 展览会

explosive n. 爆炸物

extract vt. 摘录

facilitate vt. 促进; 帮助; 使……容易

facilitator n. 帮助者; 推进者

feasibility n. 可行性

feature n. 特点

feedback n. 反馈

figure v. 计算在内; 估计

file vt. 归档

file-keeping n. 文件整理, 文件归档

flexible a. 灵活的, 可变通的

floating rate n. 浮动汇率

floor n. 发言权

forearm n. 前臂

general body 全体(与会人员)

get stuck with 忙于; 陷于

gossip n. 流言, 闲话

grab vt. 抓; 抢; 抢夺

gracious a. 和善的; 有礼貌的; 大方的

groom v. 梳洗

halo n. 光环

hectic a. 繁忙的, 忙乱的

highlight v. 强调, 突出

humble vt. 使谦恭

humiliate v. 羞辱, 使丢脸

hunt and peck (美口)看着键盘打字

iceberg n. 冰山

identical a. 同样的, 相等的

immature *a*. 不成熟的

in lieu of 代替

incorporate *v*. 合并

incur *v*. 引起,发生

inferior *a*. 低等的,劣等的,次的

initial *a*. 起初的,开始的

input *n*. 输入

inquiry number 问询电话

inspection *n*. 检查

intact *a*. 完好无缺的

integrate *v*. 成为一体,一致

interaction *n*. 配合,相互作用

internal *a*. 内的,内部的

international trade show 国际贸易展

investigate *vt*. 调查,研究

issue the invitation 发出邀请

itching *a*. 渴望的

itinerary *n*. 行程,旅程;行程表,旅行路线

jet lag 飞行时差反应

joint venture 合资企业

knack *n*. 窍门,技巧;本事,才能

know the ropes 掌握诀窍;知道内情

knowledgeable *a*. 有丰富知识的,博学的

large-scale *a*. 大规模的

lasting *a*. 持久的,恒久的

launch *v*. 发起,推出(新产品)

leaflet *n*. 传单

leisurely *ad*. 从容地,慢慢地

lengthy *a*. 漫长的,啰嗦的

light industrial product 轻工业产品

load *n*. 重担

loan *n*. 借款

location *n*. 位置、地点

magnetic *a*. 有磁性的

margin *n*. 页面空白

mark up 标高价

mashed potatoes 土豆泥

masticated *a*. 嚼碎的

maturity *n*. 成熟

memo *n*. 备忘录

memorable *n*. 值得注意的事

metropolitan *a*. 大都市的

minutes *n*. 备忘录;会议记录

modify *vt*. 改进;改善

monotone *n*. 单一的语调

motion *n*. 提议;议案

mount *v*. 配有,安装

multiply *v*. 增加,相乘

multitask *n*. 多任务;*v*. 使多任务

multi-function *n*. 多功能

mumble *v*. 咕哝

napkin *n*. 餐巾

necessity *n*. 必需品

negotiation *n*. 协商

net revenue 净收入

novelty *n*. 新颖、新奇

nuisance *n*. 令人讨厌的人(东西或行为等)

office automation 办公自动化

oil refinery 炼油厂

operational *a*. 操作的,经营的

optical fiber 光纤

overage *a*. 过老的;*n*. 过剩,过多

over-the-counter *a*. 不需要处方也可销售的

package *v*. 打包

path *n*. 小路、路径

perceive *vt*. 注意到,觉察到

perspective *n*. 想法,观点

persuasive *a*. 能说服的,善于游说的

phone tag 互相给对方电话留言

plot *v*. 制图

poker face 一本正经的面容,面无表情的人

portion *n*. 一部分

pose *vt*. 提出

postpone *vt*. 延期;推迟

potential *a*. 潜在的

preach *v*. 说教,劝诫

precaution *n*. 预防,防备,警惕

preference *n*. 偏爱,优先(权);偏爱的事物(或人)

preliminary *a*. 初步的,预备的

prescribed materials 规定的材料

prescription *n*. 处方,药方

primary *a*. 首要的;主要的;基本的

prime *a*. 首要的;最好的

priority *n*. 优先权

private branch exchange(PBX) 专用分组交换机

proceed   vi . 前进,进行

professionalism   n . 职业化,职业特征,职业行为

promotion   n . 促销;提升,升职

propose   v . 提议,建议(某事物)

prospective   a . 预期的;未来的;可能的

publicity campaign   宣传活动

publicity   n . 宣传,宣扬

purchase   n . 购买

quibble   vt . (对小的差别或分歧)争论

quotation   n . 行情,报价

rapport   n . 融洽,和谐;融洽的关系

raspberry   n . (植)覆盆子,树莓

rate sheet   收费表,价目表

reaction   n . 反应

read off   读出

real estate   房地产

receipt   n . (企业、银行等)收到的款,收据

recognize   v . 认出,识别出

recruit   vt . 招募;招聘

refer   v . 委托

refreshment   n . 点心;茶点;提神物

register   v . 登记,注册

registration   n . 登记(证);挂号

reimburse   vt . 偿还;付还

release   v . 释放

relevant   a . 有关的

rely on   依靠

remind   v . 使想起,提醒

replacement   n . 代替者

replace   vt . 取代,代替

representative   n . 代表

reputation   n . 名气,名声,声誉,声望

reschedule   vt . 重新安排时间

reserve   v . 保留,预定

resolve   v . 解决(问题)

respectively   adv . 分别地

retail   n . 零售价

revenue   n . 收入

routine   n . 例行公事

saute   v . 煎,炒(食物)

savvy   n . 常识;理解

scales   n . 台秤,磅秤

scheduled   a . 排定的,预定的

scrutiny   n . 仔细查看,监督

seal the deal   成交

secondary   a . 次要的、从属的

selling point   产品特色

seminar   n . 研讨会

sentimental   a . 感情用事的;易伤感的

setting   n . 环境,背景

shipment   n . 船运,水运;(从海路、陆路或空运的)一批货物

shorthand   n . 速记

shuttle service   班车服务

simplify   v . 简化

simultaneously   adv . 同时地

slogan   n . 口号,标语

slouch   v . 低头垂肩地站(或坐,走)

slurp   v . 饮食出声

smudge   v . 涂脏   n . 污点

snag   n . 阻碍

specialty   n . 特产,名产,特色菜

specify   vt . 详细说明;指定;阐述

splendid   a . (口语)极好的;绝妙的

spreadsheet   n . 电子数据表

stenographer   n . 速记员

storage   n . 储藏

stuffed   a . 吃饱了

styling mousse   护发定型乳剂

subcontractor   n . 转包商

submit   v . 提交;上交

subtract   v . 减

suggestion box   建议箱,意见箱

sumptuous   a . 奢侈的

superior   n . 上级;上司

supervise   vt . 监督;管理

supervisor   n . 监督者,管理者

take ... for granted   认为理所当然

take the roll call   点名

technique   n . 技巧

time-consuming   a . 耗费时间的

timer   n . 计时器

timidity   n . 腼腆

to be delayed   耽误,延误

to be engaged   忙于……

to catch a person's name   听清楚名字

to hold the line　不挂断电话

toast　*n*. 祝酒辞

toffee apples　拔丝苹果

toner cartridge　硒鼓

tough　*a*. 困难的

transaction　*n*. 交易

treasurer　*n*. 会计；出纳员

trial　*n*. 试用、试验

unappetizing　*a*. 引不起食欲的，引不起兴趣的

undivided　*a*. 专一的，专心的，全部的

unrealistic　*a*. 不现实的，不切实际的

upbeat　*a*. 积极乐观的

utilize　*v*. 利用，使用

value added tax　增值税

vehicle　*n*. 交通工具，车辆

ventilation　*n*. 空气流通；通风设备

venture　*n*. 活动，（经济）行为

venue　*n*. 会场

verification　*n*. 确认，查证

version　*n*. 版本

vibration　*n*. 震动；摆动

vigilant　*a*. 警戒的；警惕的

virtual　*a*. 实际的，实质的；（计）虚拟的

voicemail　*n*. 语音留言

warranty　*n*. 保修（期）

workload　*n*. 工作量

wreck　*v*. 毁坏

图书在版编目(CIP)数据

涉外秘书英语听说/肖爱萍,朱向荣主编.—上海:华东师范大学出版社,2013.4

高校涉外秘书专业系列教材

ISBN 978 - 7 - 5675 - 0626 - 8

Ⅰ.①涉⋯ Ⅱ.①肖⋯②朱⋯ Ⅲ.①秘书-英语-听说教学-高等学校-教材 Ⅳ.①H319.9

中国版本图书馆 CIP 数据核字(2013)第 083946 号

涉外秘书英语听说

主　　编	肖爱萍　朱向荣
策划编辑	李恒平　范耀华
项目编辑	姚　望
审读编辑	何佩建
装帧设计	卢晓红　崔　楚

出版发行　华东师范大学出版社
社　　址　上海市中山北路 3663 号　邮编 200062
网　　址　www.ecnupress.com.cn
电　　话　021 - 60821666　行政传真 021 - 62572105
客服电话　021 - 62865537　门市(邮购)电话 021 - 62869887
地　　址　上海市中山北路 3663 号华东师范大学校内先锋路口
网　　店　http://hdsdcbs.tmall.com

印 刷 者　南通印刷总厂有限公司
开　　本　787×1092　16 开
印　　张　6.75
字　　数　132 千字
版　　次　2013 年 8 月第一版
印　　次　2013 年 8 月第一次
书　　号　ISBN 978 - 7 - 5675 - 0626 - 8/H·623
定　　价　28.00 元

出 版 人　朱杰人